A STAY AT HOME DAD'S GUIDE TO RAISING STRONG GIRLS

Dr. Jon Kester

authorHOUSE®

AuthorHouse™
1663 Liberty Drive
Bloomington, IN 47403
www.authorhouse.com
Phone: 833-262-8899

Published by AuthorHouse 03/21/2023

ISBN: 979-8-8230-0416-9 (sc)
ISBN: 979-8-8230-0417-6 (hc)
ISBN: 979-8-8230-0418-3 (e)

Library of Congress Control Number: 2023905391

Print information available on the last page.

This book is printed on acid-free paper.

DEDICATION

This book is dedicated to the strong women in
my life of the past, present and future.

Grandma Alice

Sasha

Kambria "Kitty"

CONTENTS

Congratulations to all the men and women out there who are blessed to be called parents of girls and who take the time to care about how their children grow up. There is no greater privilege in life than bringing a tiny new human into this world and then trying to raise her properly during their childhood. Being a parent means to raise your daughter with the utmost love and passion so she can have a successful life. Parents must take into account that raising strong girls in today's world requires all the intelligence, wisdom, and determination they will be able to muster.

This book will help you become a wiser, more determined parent with the easy to follow month by month parenting plan. A solid, intact parenting strategy will have a significantly positive impact on your daughter's present and future wellbeing and offers countless benefits for both parents and children. In fact girls who grow up in homes where parents have strategies for success are less likely to experience a wide range of problems (academic, social, emotional, cognitive), not only in childhood but later on in adulthood as well (Amato; Howard & Reeves 2018,). In families with parenting strategies, girls typically have access to more of the economic and community resources because parents are able to pool their time, money and energy; girls tend to be more of the focus of the home.

Also girls living with a mom and dad who have parenting strategies are more often involved in community activities, take part in academic pursuits in local schools and other academic institutions that can lead to college, and eventually, a career. Girls with parents who strive for them to be strong women with a plan have the highest high school and college **graduation rates**, as well as **high employment** rates according to a study by Harvard University. Being raised in a family where parents are directly involved in the girls life reduced her probability of living in poverty by about 82 percent. (2018 PEW Research)

In order for parents to see our daughters become truly strong women, we must be involved and have a plan. Remember being an involved parent takes time and is hard work, and it often means rethinking and rearranging our priorities. It frequently means sacrificing what you want to do for what your daughter needs to do. We must be there for our girls both mentally as well as physically.

Being involved in your daughter's life has many rewards—memories, great conversations, a deeper relationship with your girl and the chance to watch your daughter grow into a healthy, responsible adult. Keep in mind that the more involved you are, the more valued your daughter feels, and the more likely she will be to respond to you.

One of the biggest challenges facing parents when it comes to being more involved with their daughter is figuring out how. The involvement can take many forms which all will be discussed in the upcoming chapters in this book. Parental actions such as being a role model, instilling good habits, being consistent in discipline, and building good relationships. This can be done by taking quality time out of our day to nurture your relationship with the girl in your life with both grace and love. The key for this books success is being able to spend quality time with your girl. What is quality time? As long as you as a parent are communicating with your daughter in an upbeat and useful way, you are spending quality time with her. P.S. just being in the same room as your daughter doesn't count. Here are some helpful ways to increase the amount of quality time you share with your daughter:

Establish together time.

Establish a regular weekly routine of doing something special with your girl. Going out for a walk, getting some ice cream, or even having a conversation while you're cleaning up after dinner can help you open your lines of communication. This is essential to raising strong girls.

Have regular family meetings.

Family meetings provide a useful forum for sharing triumphs, complaints, projects and any other topics with each other. Establish some ground rules, such as everyone gets a chance to talk without interruption, and only constructive feedback is allowed. To get resistant girls to join in, try using incentives like post-meeting ice cream.

Eat meals together as often as you can.

Family meal time provides a great opportunity to talk about the day's events, to unwind, reinforce and bond with your daughter. Studies show again and again the significant, measurable scientific proof about the positive, lifelong benefits of family meals. Family meals nourish the spirit, brain and health of all family members. Regular family meals are linked to higher grades and self-esteem. Girls who grow up sharing family meals are more likely to exhibit prosocial behavior as adults, such as sharing, fairness and respect. According to a Harvard University study (2018), with each additional family meal shared each week, adolescents are less likely to show symptoms of violence, depression and suicide, less likely to use or abuse drugs or run away, and less likely to engage in risky behavior or delinquent acts. Also both adults and children who eat at home more regularly are less likely to suffer from obesity.

Once you have the basic ideas of how to spend quality time with your daughter you are ready to take the next step of adding a specific parenting plan into your daily life. This book when used properly will be an amazing stepping stone into having strong daughters who grow up to have limitless opportunities in life.

How to use this book

If you wish to get the most out of this book, there is one indispensable requirement and that to have a deep, driving desire to raise strong girls and vigorous determination to increase your ability to parent.

This book is written with a plan for raising strong girls on a monthly basis. I encourage you to read each month rapidly at first to get a bird's eye view of the concepts and then go back and reread each section thoroughly each month and apply one or two of the concepts from the chapter to your family. Be sure to stop frequently in your reading to think over what you are reading. Ask yourself just how and when you can apply each concept to your parenting.

Read this book with a pencil, pen, magic marker, or crayon in your hand. When you come across an idea that you feel you can use, circle it or make a note by it. It is perfectly fine to write ideas down on this book or underline important sentences. In fact I have underlines some stuff already for you.

If you want to get a real, lasting benefit out of this book don't imagine that skimming through it once will suffice. After reading thoroughly, you ought to spend some time reviewing it every month. Remember that the use of these concepts can be made habitual only by a constant and vigorous review and application.

We as parents must also remember that learning is an active process. We learn by doing. So, if you desire to be a better parent and raise strong daughters then you must apply the concepts from this book every opportunity that you get. If you don't you will forget them quickly and nothing will be improved in your daughter's life. It's important to understand that attempting new ideas in your family's lifestyle will require time and persistence and daily application. Remember that understanding the role of a parent takes time. Every person has the potential to be a great parent. It does not come overnight. Also when considering the responsibilities of parenting, it's important to remember that no one is perfect. We are all human and, at times, we do make mistakes. But the important thing to teach is: we can learn by our mistakes and try to avoid making the same mistakes over-and-over again. Remember that *"Parenting is not a challenge to be solved, but a reality to be experienced"*

Good luck and Enjoy!

CHAPTER 1

JANUARY

"It is easier to build strong girls than to repair broken women." - Jon Kester

Teach girls to not waste time feeling sorry for them-self

We must teach all the young females in our life not to feel sorry for them. We must teach our daughters they are not victims because they are born female. Girls need to learn to take responsibility for their actions and outcomes, and we as parents need to make sure they have an inherent understanding of the fact that frequently "life is not fair," and that strong females don't get bogged down in the unfairness of life.

Here's the biggest fact: girls are only victims when parents allow them to be victims. In order for your daughter to be a victim, parents have to accept their excuses or their blame. I suggest that parents challenge your daughters thinking by making sure they are not blaming others actions for their own.

It's also important for your daughter to know that failing a spelling test or missing free throws in the basketball game doesn't make them a victim. Our girls must understand that failure, rejection, and disappointment are part of life.

We as parents must help our girls learn to take personal responsibility for the way they thinks, feels, and behaves. Our daughters cannot go through life insisting they are victims of "mean" people and unfortunate circumstances.

Here are some steps parents can take to empower their girls and make them lose the victim mentality:

Create "Gratefulness" Rituals

Being gratefulness keeps self-pity at bay. Spend time talking about what you're thankful for every day. Even when you encounter difficult circumstances, parents need to be role models of an appreciative attitude.

Create daily rituals that will help your daughter recognize all the reasons they have to be grateful. Here are a few ideas:

- At dinner, ask your daughter about the three favorite things that happened in school that day that they are appreciative for.
- At bedtime, ask them to tell you what the best part of their day was.
- Put pictures on the refrigerator that shows people and events that you as a family are thankful for.

Teach Your Daughter to Silence their Destructive Thinking

Some girls tend to have a more pessimistic outlook than others. But with a little help, they can recognize their negative thinking may not be accurate.

Help your daughter silence their negative thinking by looking for exceptions to the rule. If they insists, "I don't ever get to do anything fun," remind them of the fun activities they recently participated in. If your daughter says, "No one ever likes me," point out people who do. Remember as a parent your attitude is often times reflexed on to your child's thinking and now will be a good time to self-evaluate to make sure your outlook on life is positive.

Teach Your Daughter How to Deal with Unpleasant Emotions

We as parents must teach our daughters how to deal with uncomfortable emotions, like fear, anxiety, anger, and sadness. According child phycologist, Dr. Diana Paulson, girls who have healthy coping skills are less likely to insist minor events are catastrophic which can result in depression.

Discipline your daughter's behavior, but not the emotion. Let your daughter know that their emotions are OK, but that it's important to handle those emotions in appropriate manners. Our girls need to know healthy ways to express their feelings and not always have their own pity party every time they get upset.

A girl who has confidence in their ability to handle disappointment won't lament that life isn't fair when it's time to leave the playground, or when they don't make the basketball team.

Teach Problem-Solving Skills

According to David Owens from the National institute of learning, Kids who lack problem-solving skills are likely to take a passive approach to life. A child who doesn't know how to do their math homework may resign to a failing grade without even trying to find a solution. Or, a child who doesn't make the soccer team may conclude they are a terrible athlete.

As parents we must teach our daughters how to problem-solve. A girl who takes action when they face hardship is much less likely to see themselves as a helpless victim. Remember that females with good problem-solving skills can prevent small stumbling blocks from turning into major obstacles.

Help Other People

It's easy for girls to think they have the biggest problems in the world. Showing them that there are plenty of other people with bigger problems can help them see that everyone faces hardships. Helping other people can show your daughter that no matter how young they are, or no matter what problems they experienced, they have the ability to help someone else.

Volunteer at a homeless shelter, help an elderly neighbor with yard work or participate in a fundraising project. Get your daughter involved in community service activities on a regular basis so they can recognize opportunities to make the world a better place.

Teach Assertiveness Skills

As parents we must teach our daughters that they don't have to be a passive victim. If another child grabs a toy from their hand, help them ask for it back. Or, if they are being picked on by other kids at school, talk about how to ask a teacher for help.

Girls with assertiveness skills can speak up and say, "Don't do that," or "I don't like it when you do that." Empower your daughter to use their words and you'll reduce the likelihood that they become a victim.

Final Though

We as parents need to know that when girls take on a victim mentality, it becomes a form of defiance, used to avoid taking appropriate responsibility for their actions. If left unchanged, the victim mentality can eventually impact your daughter ability to have healthy relationships and to adequately function as an adult. It is vital that the girl in your life learns the skills discussed in this section in order to manage their accountability in the real world and then will be one step closer to becoming strong women.

Surround girls with positive role models of BOTH genders

Over the last twenty years or maybe even longer some parts of society push that the only way to raise strong women is for girls to have powerful female role models. Strong women role models for sure contribute to girls growing up to be amazing women. However, I may be bias but Dads and men also play an equal role in the shaping of strong girls. We need to encourage father/daughter bonds (or grandfathers, uncles, and so on) so they grow up seeing how women deserve to be treated. We need to show our daughters that strong men and strong women can work side by side and do great things like run businesses, the government or most importantly raising a family.

In today's current "politically correct" culture it is way too easy to villainize men and make them the enemy, but you're not doing your daughter any favors by doing so. It's also incredibly unfair to our sons. Equality, by its very definition, bars us from declaring the opposite sex our enemy. After all, very few would see their enemy as an equal. So, show your girls that there are just as many wonderful male role models as there are females and that it's okay to look up to them, too. When this occurs your daughter will be one step closer to being truly strong!

Limit your daughter's exposure to the social media when she is young

In today's society our girls cannot get away from social media and popular culture. It's at playgrounds, restaurants, in cars, at schools, — basically everywhere. According to Jenny Radesky from psmagazine. com, when girls' attention is directed at a social media, they talk to their peers less, miss learning cues, overreact when interruption occur, and think less clearly about what their behavior means.

According to Diane Levine, author of So Sexy SO Soon says that limiting girl's exposure to social media will give her more time to develop her own ideas, creativity, and imagination from her direct first-hand experience. "As she grows, media messages will start to get in, so having rules and routines from the start can help your daughter control her own experiences as she gets older," Below are some suggestions on how to control social media with your daughter at any age.

Have family discussion about appropriate social media use

The first step for parents to take in order to control social media is to have discussion about their use with their daughter. Even young girls can contribute to a conversation about social media use around the house. This will help them understand why social media can be both a positive and negative thing. It will also help them understand why you set rules on their technology usage. Ask them what they think appropriate electronic media use looks like and what sorts of consequences might be warranted for breaking the agreed-upon rules. You may have to help guide them in these discussions, but often you'll find that they have expectations that are not that different from your own

Consider Habit Triggers

In The Power of Habit, Charles Duhigg wrote "Most of the choices we make every day may feel like the products of well-considered decision making, but they're not."

Many times girls automatically reach for their phones or go to the computer in certain situations to check social media. Try to pay attention to these cues or triggers. When do they automatically reach for their phone? What can they do differently during those times, besides look at the phone? Or how can our daughter change the way their social media and phones using their phone. For example, find a video about a school topic on social media then engage in conversation about what you saw with your daughter. Again this will be different depending on the age of the girl in your life.

Make Family rules

Once you have good conversations with your children and figured out the reasons to use / not use social media then rules must be established. Some example of rules that could be made are as followed:

- No social media for the first hour after coming home
- No social media for adults until the kids are in bed
- No social media during meals (for sure!!)
- No social media during a family movie

Parents, make sure you designate a spot or drawer where you will stash your phone during the rules period.

Final thoughts

As parents we must take into account that intense attention our daughters devote to social media has a major, measurable impact on their health, wellbeing, and most importantly their family relationships. We must create healthy social media boundaries. These boundaries should be something that we should all hope our kids might inherit and follow outside of your home, and may even pass down to their own kids someday.

CHAPTER 2

FEBRUARY

"Be that strong girl that everyone knew would make it through the worst, be that fearless girl, the one who would dare to do anything". – Taylor swift

Strong girls do not worry about pleasing others

We must teach our daughters that they simply cannot please everyone with their actions. According to Dr. Rhonda Johnson writer of Girl Power 2.0, girls for some reason have an inherit ant idea that they must try to make people happy all day, every day. We as parents need to make sure the girls in our lives know that there's nothing wrong with being nice or kind to someone else. In fact, it's a pretty valuable trait. But it can also be something we do to avoid disappointing others or put pressure on ourselves to live up to an <u>ideal image</u>. A lot of females consciously choose to act this way because they are afraid of upsetting others. It is a great way to avoid conflict, but in the long run it will leave them feeling drained and unhappy. I personally feel that it's hard to be true to yourself when you're always changing your actions and words based on what you think other people want.

According to Dr. Paula McCafferty, many females find it easy to focus the majority of their energy on pleasing other people rather than focusing on providing themselves with happiness. As a result, this kind of behavior inevitably causes low self-esteem, feeling like there are too many expectations on them, and then in turn the development of poor coping skills occur.

Here are 5 tips that we can use to help our daughters to not be constant people pleasures:

Be true to yourself instead of trying to fit in.

The most important thing we can do is to teach our daughters is to stay true to their self. Girls need to avoid doing something just because it'll make them look good in someone else's eyes, and stick to what they know is right for them . As parents, it is our responsibility to make sure they are taught that if they are ever put on the spot and asked to do something that they don't feel comfortable with, they shouldn't be afraid to stand their ground. It shows that they are strong enough to make their own decisions.

Learn to say "NO"

Sometimes people-pleasing can become such a deeply ingrained habit that girls have to tell themselves that it is okay to say "no". It's okay to put yourself first and say "no" if someone asks you for something you don't want to do, or if they ask you for something unreasonable or impossible. You also need to stop saying "yes" when you not getting anything out of the task at hand and are just doing it because the other person is asking you for help.

The most important part about this is reminding yourself that saying "no" when you mean it isn't being selfish, it's taking care of yourself.

Set healthy boundaries.

Girls are often unaware of the boundaries they need to set in their lives. This might seem difficult at first, but it is important that your daughter start noticing what is happening and identify things that need to change. Sit down with her and make a list of the things they are doing that makes them feel unhappy or used, like doing math homework for a friend, and rank them in order of importance with the most significant items on top.

This simple strategy can allow them to remain true to their self without feeling the need to please everyone. Boundaries give them the ability to say "no" when another person asks for help or takes advantage of their time.

Stop making excuses.

The moment your daughter stops making excuses, she'll have more time and energy to do what she really wants to do. She will feel more in control of her life and less of a victim to other people's demands.

If you make an excuse every time someone asks you to do something for them -- as in "Sorry, I'm afraid I can't do it, because..." -- then it can lead to a lack of work-life balance and leave little time for personal pursuits. (In other words: You'll get burned out.) It also means that people will start taking advantage of your good nature -- and there's nothing more frustrating than being used and taken advantage of!

Listen to your inner voice.

Life is a journey, and on that journey our daughters will meet many people who will want things from her. Your daughter may find herself becoming someone else's doormat in order to get someone to like them. The problem with this is that it will stop them from being able to be happy and make their own decisions.

If your daughter wants to stop being a people-pleaser, then she needs to start listening to what her inner voice is telling her. This voice may be telling her that certain people are toxic and that they aren't worth it.

Final thoughts

Worrying about trying to please others is not a healthy way of living and it can lead to feelings of exhaustion, stress, and even depression. It's important that our daughters learn to control their life and know that they are important too. People-pleasing can start to feel like a habit and difficult to break out of. But with time, patience, and perseverance, anything is possible.

Help Her Feel Unique

According to a study by the American Association of Phycology at Brown University a girl's self-esteem drops 3.5 times more than a boy's during the period between 5th grades to their senior year of high school. The antidote? Encourage your young daughter's individuality, and you'll lay a foundation that will be her emotional scaffolding as she enters the trickier tween and teen years. "Adolescence is when girls truly start to understand their identity as separate from their parents, so they will experiment with various types like the 'class clown' or the 'renegade,' "explains Dr. Radin. But if they already have a strong sense of self, they have a much easier time navigating adolescence."

Here are some recommendations for how parents can continue to get to know their children and help truly find what makes their daughter unique.

Discover

Cast a wide net when encouraging your daughter to discover her passions. During a trip to the library, don't nudge her toward books about tea parties. Even if she's the girly-girl type, who's to say she wouldn't also love a book about football? Instead of signing her up for gymnastics because it's the popular choice, present a range of options and see what she picks maybe mixed martial arts. Once she shows an interest in something, give her lots of chances to explore it. It's key to help her hone her interests when they're different from the rest of the family's. "Some girls have obvious gifts, but others (like, say, the child who isn't so coordinated in a family of natural athletes) need help drawing them out," says Dr. Silverman. "I once worked with a soccer-player mom whose daughter had no interest in the sport, but she loved swimming and flourished once her mom put her on the swim team. It seems obvious, but it can be hard for moms when they aren't the mentor. Instead, realize that sometimes you'll be the bridge who connects your daughter to the expert."

Just remember to take time each day to observe your child up close and from afar. Look for changes. Look for new skills. Experience your child as a person by interacting with them.

Listen and Ask Questions

Discovery includes truly listening to your child. It means inquiring about how they think and feel about all aspects of their life. The more you can listen with openness and acceptance, the more you will discover and at the same time affirm your daughter as a unique individual. Questions should be asked for the purpose of learning more. Find out what lead them to those feelings and thoughts, and how long they've held those thoughts or feelings. This is the time to show interest and understanding, provide support, and volunteer guidance but only if requested or when it raises serious concerns.

Observe and Comment

This is the fun part of parenting – watching your child be a kid. Where they're playing a game, drawing, playing music, performing, learning a new skill, showing off a physical feat or attempting comedy, all you have to do is watch, enjoy, and celebrate with a smile, applause, and a pat on the back. Provide praise and encouragement. Avoid being a critic – that's the job of teachers and coaches, and your children will surely get criticism from peers as well.

Engage In Child-Directed Play

Playing is good for people of all ages. It reduces stress, promotes health, and is just plain fun. When playing with younger kids as well as older children and teens, let them direct the play. Join in and have fun. Let toddlers and preschoolers make up the rules for games if they want. Get in touch with your inner child and enjoy along with them.

Expose Your Daughter To Many Different Activities

Girls should be exposed to all types of opportunities to try new things such as sports, music, art, drama, science, reading, visiting parks, the forest, the beach, museums, hobbies, and anything else you can think of. Encourage them to give it a try. Praise them for trying new things. If they become interested, encourage them and support them in their pursuit. If they feel like giving up after a while, find out why and encourage them to keep going when things get harder or they become bored or lose interest. At some point we as parents may have to let them quit even when we think they could be successful at the endeavor. Letting them quit without a huge struggle and letting them know the door is always open is the best way to go.

Show Patience and Understanding

No matter the situation, patience and understanding are always good to maintain. While dealing with children can be frustrating, being patient and showing that you understand how they are feeling helps a lot. Try to model and coach patience along with encouragement in the affirming of their abilities. Talk them through the process step by step and cheer them along the way.

Conclusion

God made everyone in their own unique way. As parents it is our jobs to insure our daughter embrace their talents and gifts. When this occurs the girls in our lives will truly be strong.

Teach your daughter to laugh everyday

Humor is one of a number of things — like art or dramatic play — that Girls can create at a young age and has astronomical effects on their life. According to Dr. Jean Conrad Humor fosters a relaxed and playful climate in which further creativity is more likely to occur. "Humor, creativity, playfulness, and play are closely connected, so a home or classroom that's conducive to any of them is likely to have an abundance of all of them and be filled with the laughter of happy girls." (Conrad, 2011)

Here are some simple tips to get your girl giggling.

> **Maintain a warm, supportive atmosphere in your home**. Remember, a girl who feels that not only her humor, but her very self is likely to be ridiculed isn't likely to have the confidence to risk silliness.

> **Be playful with your Girl.** Physical comedy is particularly popular with young children (lap games, odd timing, peculiar body language, gestures, and facial expressions). As children begin experimenting with and mastering language, verbal play is always a smash hit. Encourage imagination and pretend play, curiosity, ideas, and originality.

Build your daughters self-esteem in all aspects of her life — physical and social accomplishments, competence, and knowledge. A constricted, inhibited girl with low self-esteem is rarely very good at creating or appreciating humor.

Help your daughter become aware of the needs, wishes, and pleasures of other children. To amuse peers, a child has to understand their perspective and mood somewhat and be able to move in tune with his audience. When we help a child learn to solve problems with siblings and friends by listening, explaining, negotiating, and acting on the solution they've agreed to, we're working on the foundation essential for a sense of humor, as well as for so much else.

Use humors you in everyday life. Show the way by introducing a bit of nonsense in tense situations between children. In addition to teaching children problem-solving skills, guide them in relating to peers with a twinkle when it feels as if a light touch would reduce the level of anger, aggression, or anxiety in the air.

Share stories that tickle her funny bones. Try stories with illustrations, incidents, and entanglements that are incongruous with the way your child knows things really are.

Throw in a pinch of laughter when a child's compliance is needed but lacking. This can increase the likelihood that the adult's objective will be met, everyone will come out unscathed, and the child will have more respect for the adult's ability to be a fun person. For instance: "The bath toys are still in the tub? The tub alarm's going off! Bleep! Bleep! Oh, put the toys away, stop this horrible racket! Hurry! Oh, thank goodness, you stopped that awful alarm! Tomorrow, try to remember to get the bath toys out before you get out."

Let your daughter feel superior and laugh at you. Turn the tables now and then. Make goofy mistakes to give your daughter a chuckle. This can add balance to the incontrovertible fact that you are, and you should be, the boss. On the other hand, don't let the big kids scoff at the little kids. Older children are so relieved to know that they've grown that they tend to ridicule younger ones (children who represent what they were very recently).

Make a joke out of making a mistake. One of the most useful tools in the mental health toolbox, and for achieving social success, is the ability to laugh good-naturedly at oneself. It's hard not to like a cheerful child and one who makes you laugh, so peers are less likely to "mean tease" a child who teases about his own oddities and errors.

Provide your child with the structure she needs to be able to predict what you expect. Reasonable household policies (call them rules if you prefer) and a schedule (albeit flexible) help children "act right." Being able to manage one's behavior is part of being able to use humor judiciously. A child who inflicts her rowdiness on a sibling or friend without sensitivity to his wishes is not a skilled humorist.

Final Thoughts

The ability to appreciate humor enriches a girl's life in all dimensions. By using humor, girls feel free to deviate from the rules. Laughter is an expression of freedom from the way things really are, and we can all occasionally use a little escape from the way things really are! – True Story

CHAPTER 3

MARCH

"A girl should be two things: who and what she wants." – Coco Channel

Strong girls do not give away their power

For our girls not to give away their power this basically means they need to avoid giving others the power to make them feel inferior or bad about themselves. Our daughters need to learn how to put up some boundaries and not let others words hurt them, especially if it isn't true. Remember that other people's words affect us because we don't like to be judged, so we constantly worry about what people think and say about us and carefully curate the image we want to portray to the world.

But as human beings, we all have different principles, beliefs, and values, and throughout our lifetime, we inevitably meet people with different points of view, thoughts, or opinions. This can lead to conflict and disagreement if you care too much what other people think of you. But caring too much about what others think is disempowering — it gives others power over our daughters and has the potential to hold them back from doing something that's important to them.

The Females in our life can follow these tips in order to insure that other people's words do not affect them so much.

No-One Can take Your Power Without consent

The first thing to remember when someone says something hurtful to you is that they are only words, which can't survive if you don't let them. According to Bijan Kholghi, Humans have analytical minds that tend to take on board the words of others and assimilate them into our own negative self-talk. This becomes a vicious cycle which feeds your insecurities, fears, worries, and anger and can negatively affect your wellbeing."

Fortunately, it's possible to break this cycle by reminding yourself that they are just thoughts. A good way to do this is to bring awareness to your negative thoughts and then challenge them. When a negative thought comes up, notice it and ask yourself whether it's true and if there is any evidence or basis for this belief. Usually, you will find there is none. Then, ask yourself where this belief came from. You may well realize it came not from your own mind, but from something someone said to or about you.

Stand Up For Yourself

We do not want our daughter in a situation where someone said something about them that they didn't like, but they didn't say anything to defend themselves. The females in our lives need to know that standing up for yourself isn't easy, but it's worth it. This simple action will help them to get rid of internal negativity and increase your self-confidence and mental toughness — which will make them more resilient to other people's opinions in the future.

Personal Interpretations

Our daughters must recognize we all have different meanings and values we place on certain words — my personal interpretation of a particular word may be different from yours. Words can bring up different emotions depending on the situation, your upbringing, or memories associated with that word. If a certain word triggers you, try to be aware of the causes, and be open to the possibility that the other person didn't intend to offend you.

Don't Take It Personally

Our daughters need to be taught that when a person says something negative that affects their feelings, try not to take it personally. According to Dr. John McGluery, Often, it's more a reflection of that person than it is of you — people who are unhappy or frustrated may snap at you because they are experiencing negative emotions that make them feel upset or uncomfortable. Remember that if someone hurts others it's because they themselves are hurting, but don't know how to deal with it — doing so can help prevent their words from affecting you.

Remove Toxic People

Our daughters deserve peace and joy in their life. We must teach them that they have no obligation to share their life with people who bring you down, steal your vital energy, or look down on them. If there's someone in your daughter's life they don't like, they have every right to remove them and make space for more positive people.

According to a 2018 Harvard study, "We" are the sum of the five people you spend most time with, so our daughters must surrounding them self with positive and enriching people.

Conclusion

If there is one lesson that all parents should teach their daughters it would be doesn't worry about what other people think of you, particularly people that don't know you. Take the time and really make sure that the girls in your life know that only what they think of their self truly matters. When this occurs they truly will be strong!

Teach your Girl to enjoy Nature and all its Beauty

When I was a kid, the warm weather had me racing out the door as soon as I woke up. I usually didn't meander in through the back door again until the sun began to set and the mosquitoes began to bite. On a snowy Saturday, I would suit up, grab a sled, and search out the nearest hill, staying out until my fingers and toes were numb. Rainy days didn't deter my outdoor adventures. In fact, they packed all sorts of new ones. What kid doesn't love to splash in puddles?

Unfortunately, so many kids these days haven't even experienced the joy of riding their bikes in the rain or exploring the nearby woods. Freely playing outside for hours at a time simply isn't done often anymore. We as parents need to make sure our girls to enjoy nature.

The girls in our live should not only enjoy nature because of its beauty but also because of some of the following amazing benefits of doing so.

BENEFITS OF SPENDING TIME WITH NATURE

Best source of Vitamin D. Supplements have nothing on sunshine. Vitamin D is incredibly important for preventing chronic diseases and even reducing certain cancer risks! With all-natural vitamin D, you'll also strengthen your bones, prevent diabetes, and lower your risk of developing Alzheimer's.

Promotes a natural sleep pattern. With the artificial light we're constantly exposed to throughout our days, our bodies get confused about when it's time to wind down and sleep. When you spend regular time outdoors, your body clock begins to adjust to a natural pattern, thus giving you a better night's sleep.

Increases brain function. Studies have found that nature can reduce the symptoms of ADHD in children. Adults benefit in a similar way. Even admiring a natural view through a window or in a painting can amp up productivity and concentration. If you're struggling with tackling that next big project, take a walk through a park because nature also enhances creativity.

Boosts immunity. The Japanese call it forest bathing. When you spend time outdoors regularly, you'll elevate the level of white blood cells in your blood. These white blood cells fight infection and tumor cells. You may also lower your blood pressure with a jaunt through the woods.

Reduces stress and anxiety. Nature just makes us happier. Our bodies slow down when we spend time in nature, reducing the production of the stress hormone, cortisol. The outdoors can improve your mood and even boost your self-esteem. Take a weekend camping trip, and the stress relieving benefits will pour into the rest of your week.

There are literally tons of actives you and your girls can do to enjoy nature. Here are some simple ideas that every parent should take into consideration on a daily basis:

Take a Hike.

Get outside and just have fun exploring your local forest. This is our favorite thing to do in the spring and fall especially, when the forest is starting to re-grow in the spring after winter, and then again in the fall when leaves are changing color and starting to fall off. If you live in a milder climate, you'll have wonderful hiking weather all through the year – lucky you! We often collect items on our hikes, like K's personal favorite, sticks, as well as any cool branches we see for craft projects and items to add to our nature table, like pinecones, fallen feathers and cool leaves and rocks. Look out for local birds and other creatures like deer, squirrels, caterpillars and butterflies.

Ride Your Bikes.

I still remember meeting up with friends in the neighborhood on a warm summer's day and riding our bikes around. K has a cool little Strider bike that he just loves and he can zip around pretty quickly on it, keeping up with us. We also have a carrier that he can sit in (it fits 2 kids too) and is perfect for longer bike rides. Just being out in the fresh air and being able to get to your destination on a bike instead of having to pile into the car is so refreshing.

Go Camping.

There's nothing like spending 24/7 in the elements. Pack up the tent and hit your favorite camping spot. Most kids love the novelty of cooking over an open campfire, wandering through the forest, swimming at the local lake or ocean (if the site is near a body of water), and sleeping outside in a tent. There is so much to learn from living more simply this way and even if it is only temporarily, it really helps you get more connected to Mother Nature.

Spend a Day at the Beach.

One of our all-time favorite things to do is pack up a cooler of healthy drinks, snacks and lunch, grab a few beach toys and other necessities and hit the beach for the day. Building sand castles, splashing in the water, lying in the sand, taking walks on the beach, collecting shells and other beach goodies....there is so much to do! I don't know any kid that doesn't love the beach and spending a day here will teach kids to love nature and help connect them with the natural element of water.

Garden Together.

Teach children all about where our food comes from by getting them started early in the garden. Start seeds inside together if necessary and then let kids help dig the holes and plant the seeds or seedlings. If you have space, give your child a small plot of their own to grow whatever they would like in it and tend to it themselves. It's so rewarding growing your own food and showing children the evolutionary process of a seed to a full vegetable or fruit is pretty amazing. This will definitely get them to appreciate nature.

Take up Seasonal Outdoor Activities.

To get the most out of each season, try to find activities or sports that each child loves and enjoys doing. Winter activities include skiing, skating and hockey, as well as fun things like tobogganing. There's swimming in the summer, as well as soccer and baseball as soon as the weather warms up, and of course, bike riding. K started playing soccer last year and is super excited to play again this year. It's totally just for fun but that's the way it should be at his age and the little ones love it.

Go Fruit Picking.

Picking local fruit is one of our favorite things to do all season long, beginning with strawberries. We pick as many as we can so that we can freeze bags and enjoy them throughout the year in smoothies and baked goods. Kids can be a big help once they're old enough to pick as well, and you can even wear the littlest ones. Fruit picking gets you outside and shows children where the fruit they eat comes from and how it's grown. Bonus: you can snack while you pick!

Respect the Earth and Creatures.

Teach children to respect nature and all its creatures. Learning about the animals and what they eat, where they hibernate and where they live gives children a better understanding of the animals' place in the world. Trees are also a thing of awe and beauty since they provide us with oxygen, shade and food. Just by naturally pointing out what each element does really helps kids appreciate the natural world. I realized this recently when we drove by a bunch of trees that had just been cut down to expand a roadway and my daughter Kitty pointed them out, saying "Those trees are so sad to be cut down. We should plant new ones."

Bring the Outside In

Start a nature table or use small baskets to hold natural elements from outside. We have a small table that we use to welcome each season and we place little items their each season such as pinecones, beach shells, and handmade items like eggs in a basket for Easter or beeswax candles for winter. Since K is big into collecting items from outside (like many kids are), we also have some baskets in our play area specifically for smaller sticks, rocks and stones, and other fun items. We have a big stick collection at the front door as well as he likes to pick up a new walking stick on each hike. You can also use items you find to make nature crafts.

Final Thoughts

Whenever you can, just get outside. I'll be the first to admit that I am a Fall person, but trying to enjoy every season for what it offers (snow covered trees in a forest are absolutely beautiful as well) can help ensure you get outside as much as possible, even if it's for a quick walk on those cold winter days. Try to walk or bike to your destinations as much as possible. Schedule playdates at local parks or ask friends to meet up for an outdoor hike or walk with your daughter instead of sitting inside. Enjoy that fresh air and oxygen and your daughter will naturally learn to love and connect with nature. After all a girl who connects with nature will truly be one step closer to becoming strong!

Let her know it's okay to ask for help

The fact is that part of being strong is knowing when you need a little help. So, while you're teaching your daughter to stand up for herself, remind her that you'll be there to support her if she needs it at the same time. Life is full of ups and downs and sometimes we just need help from others.

Being able to ask for help is an essential skill for everyday life, but one that often has a stigma attached to it. It's natural for strong girls to want to "do it themselves," especially when they see adults accomplishing the same tasks without help. Asking for help can sometimes be seen as a sign of weakness or incompetence, especially as our daughters get into their teen years. According to a study by the University of Idaho, help-seeking in girls promotes positive psychological functioning, competence, and inspires healthy collaboration with the children and adults around them. When girls learn to ask for help, not only do they utilize their problem-solving skills, but they also become more adept at communicating and expressing their needs.

Help Seeking Skill

It may seem obvious to us, but asking for help can be a crucial tool to help our daughters deal with tough problems such as bullying, trouble with school work, conflict with peers, and more. In addition, help-seeking is a skill that can combat many of the risk factors that have been known to cause stress and sadness in girls. Discussing what asking for help looks like in different settings (e.g. school, home, sports team) can help ensure that our daughters can identify adults and peers who are safe and can provide them with the appropriate forms of assistance.

Of course, there's a line between encouraging help-seeking and allowing our daughters to become dependent on help. Girls should still be encouraged to try things on their own when it is safe and appropriate for them to do so, but being comfortable asking for help when it would be beneficial is a key developmental skill. Being mindful about that line can make a huge difference in your daughter's journey to becoming a strong person.

What Parents Can Do

There are many things we can do to encourage help-seeking behaviors in our daughters. One of the first steps is letting them know that you are there to help them when needed. This should be easy for most girls since they already been asking you for help since they were toddlers, and it can help to point out what that looked like as they have grown. You may have helped teach them how to walk, helped them with coloring, or helped them learn how to ride a bicycle. You can also give them examples of when you have had to ask for help in your own life to emphasize that people of all ages sometimes need help.

The following questions can aid parents and teachers in helping girls navigate how to ask for help appropriately:

- What are some things you can do without asking for help?
- What are some things you still need help with?
- How can you ask for help?

Have some suggestions ready in case your daughter needs help coming up with ideas.

Identify Potential Helpers

This can start simply by asking daughters to identify potential helpers at home, at school, and in the neighborhood. This also gives parents a chance to establish clear boundaries for appropriate individuals to approach for help.

A useful activity to promote help-seeking is to introduce girls to the individuals you have identified. Parents can take their daughters to visit neighbors, community members, and family they trust to go over topics that they can help them with. A simple exercise could be to walk over to a trusted neighbor's home and ask for a cup of sugar to bake a cake, or to borrow a shovel to remove snow from the drive way. This presents a great opportunity for your daughter to practice asking for help in a comfortable, low-stakes situation. It also gives you a chance to talk about healthy boundaries afterwards. Although we can ask the neighbor for a cup of sugar, we probably shouldn't also be asking them for the flour, milk, and eggs! We can ask the neighbor to use their rake, but once we are done we have to give it back to them in the same condition we received it.

Knowing who not to ask for help can be equally important, and those boundaries should be clearly established as well. Emphasize that they should only approach and request help from known, trusted adults (or kids!). Many girls should already know this, but it can be helpful to reiterate, especially as we're asking them to brainstorm a list of people that they can approach.

Model Help-Seeking at Home

Help-seeking can be modeled in your home, too! If your daughter has a sibling, perhaps they can ask for help with picking up toys. You can ask your daughter to help you with a house chore, or even something fun, like baking cookies. It's important to stress that, while of course you can do more things on your own as you get older, no one is ever too old to ask for help.

Final thoughts

Asking for help is a basic, important skill, but is one that both we as parents and our daughters often don't utilize enough! Encouraging girls at a young age to be independent but also comfortable asking for help sets them up for success down the road and becoming truly strong! PS - it's okay to be fierce and strong yet still need your dad sometimes.

CHAPTER 4

APRIL

"I alone cannot change the world, but I can cast a stone across the water to create many ripples." — Mother Teresa

Teach Her to Not Waste Energy on Things She Cannot Control

One of the major causes of weakness in our daughters occurs when she spends the majority of her energy on things she cannot control. When our girls do this she pulls her energy away from what she can do something about. For example, a girl with fat parents cannot do anything about the obesity gene that runs in her family, but she can exercise regularly and make better eating choices. We must teach our daughter not to focus on what she can't change but put their energy into what they can.

Here are three things that can help the females in our life learn to not waste their time on things she cannot control.

1. Determine what they can control.

We need to teach our daughters to take a minute to examine the things they have control over. For example they can't prevent a storm from coming but they can prepare for it. At the same time your daughter can't control how someone else behaves, but they can control how they react.

They need to recognize that sometimes, all they can control is their effort and their attitude.

2. Focus on their influence.

Our daughters need to understand that they can influence people and circumstances, but they can't force things to go their way. So while you can give your child the tools he needs to get good grades, you can't make her get a 4.0 GPA. And while you can plan a good birthday party, you can't make people have fun.

The girls in our lives need to learn that in order to have the most influence, focus on changing their behavior. They need to be a good role model and set healthy boundaries for themselves.

When they have concerns about someone else's choices, make sure they share their opinion, but only share it once. Don't try to fix people who don't want to be fixed.

3. Differentiate between ruminating and problem-solving.

Replaying conversations in your head or imagining catastrophic outcomes over and over again isn't helpful. But solving a problem is. So we must help are daughter's determine whether their thinking is productive. If they are actively solving a problem, such as trying to find ways to increase their chances of success, then this form of thinking needs to condition. However, me must make sure our daughters are not wasting their time ruminating. If this occurs then the girls in our lives need to acknowledge that their thoughts aren't productive and get up and go do something for a few minutes to get their brain focused on something more constructive.

Conclusion

Once our daughters learn the difference between things they can and can't not control then they will be truly strong. They will be able to determine whether they need to take action and make something happen or calm down in order to deal with the things they have no control over.

Don't Worry About Failure

You might be surprised to learn that letting your daughter screw up is one of the best ways to build her confidence. According to Dr. Sarah Pace, girls are inadvertently groomed to become perfectionists by being praised for "good girl" behavior, so they quickly learn that making mistakes means "not good enough." This becomes problematic because researchers have found that it's the very process of taking risks and messing up that builds confidence, explains Katy Kay, lead anchor of BBC World News America and coauthor of *The Confidence Code.* "We tend to make our kids' lives easy by doing things for them because we're so desperate for them to succeed. But then when you tell a child she can do 'anything,' she has no evidence to support that because she hasn't had to work hard at anything," says Kay.

It's sad to say but for many girls the fear of failure can be crippling and make them give up even before they try something new. According to Child phycologist, Dr. Jason Peterman, the fear of failure among girls in America today is at epidemic proportions. The fear of failure causes girls to experience debilitating anxiety before they take a test, compete in a sport, or perform in a recital. The fear of failure causes our children to give less than their best effort, not take risks, and, ultimately, never achieve complete success.

The Value of Failure

We must teach our daughters that failure is an inevitable-and essential-part of life. Failure must be taught as something that can bolster the motivation to overcome the obstacles we as humans face every day. Failure can also be a valuable learning tool by connecting a girls actions with consequences, which can help them gain ownership of their efforts. According to children's psychologist, Dr. Kenneth Silvestri, failure teaches important life skills, such as commitment, patience, determination, decision making, and problem solving. Failures can also help children respond positively to the frustration and disappointment that they will often experience as they pursue their goals. Failure teaches children humility and appreciation for the opportunities that they're given.

Have Conversations about Success and Failure

As parents the first step in teaching our daughters to deal with failure is to make sure we are having conversations about the topic. Now when girls are smaller this conversation can be very simple and should focus on trying and how it is ok to fail. Once girls are in second grade or older then the conversation can get more complex and then it is encouraged to use example from your own life or from famous people such as Abe Lincoln who lost many local elections before becoming president or Michael Jordan who did not make his varsity basketball team as a sophomore. Remember to explain that failure can be beneficial because it leads to success (when we learn from it and try again). Your child should know that when you fail, you learn about what works and what doesn't, you improve, and you learn to keep going instead of giving up.

Parents must lead by example:

One of the main themes of raising strong daughters is to be a role model, so we as parents must always remember that our daughters learn from our example. Stanford University researchers Carol Dweck and Kyla Haimovitz have found that kids learn their attitudes about failure from their parents. By watching their parents, girls develop one of two ideas: that failure is "enhancing" or that failure is "debilitating." When we as parents fail try to respond with positivity or humor. Be sure that you talk to your daughter about what you've learned from your mistakes (whether past or present), and how you picked yourself up and tried again.

Emphasize Effort, Not Ability

When our girls are trying anything new we must first and foremost emphasize giving 100 percent effort. History is full example of people having tons of ability and ending up wasting it or losing out to people who give more effort. Demonstrate that performance is not about ability. It's about effort, practice, learning strategies, and determination.

Carol Dweck of Stanford University and her colleagues studied hundreds of 5th grade children, praising one group for their *abilities* and the other for their *efforts*. Both groups were challenged with a difficult test designed for 8th grade students. The group who was praised for their effort tried very hard, although they naturally made plenty of mistakes. The group who was praised for intelligence became discouraged when they made mistakes, seeing these errors as a lack of ability and a sign of failure. Overall, intelligence testing for the "effort "group increased by 30%, while it decreased by 20% for the "ability" group, all because of different attitudes about mistakes and failure.

This doesn't mean you should simply tell your daughter to "Try harder," when they struggle (especially if they have truly made an effort). But you can discuss specific strategies that might work next time, rather than saying something ability-oriented like, "its okay if you aren't strong enough to play football."

Help focus on the Solution

Instead of telling your daughter to give up on gymnastics because she is not strong enough, as a parent you need to help your kid focus on a solution to get better. The first step is discussing what went wrong or why did your kid fail. The second step to help kids focus on the solution is to find out how to fix or prevent what went wrong for the next time. Make sure that you let your child brainstorm solutions, but you can also make suggestions, such as, "Do you think it would help to join a gym and start lifting weights to get stronger for gymnastics?

By helping your daughter focus on the solution you're teaching your child not to respond to failures with frustration, disappointment, or giving up. They will learn that failure simply means going back to the drawing board and devising new, better approaches and strategies.

Demonstrate Unconditional Love

According to UC Berkeley professor Matt Covington, the fear of failure is directly linked to your self-worth, or to the belief that you are valuable as a person. Girls usually tie their self-worth to what their parents think about them. They might feel their parents won't love or appreciate them as much if they don't maintain high grades, superb athletic or artistic performance, perfect behavior, etc. Naturally, this belief results in a fear of failure.

As parents it's a given that we love our children unconditionally but be sure to tell them that. Our children need to know that even if they make mistakes or fail at something we love them no matter what the results are. Also be sure that your children know they don't have to be perfect at everything, its ok to get a few answers wrong on a math test or strike out in baseball.

Final thoughts

Parents let's make our girls strong by making sure they are able to accept failure. Remember to explain that you will *always* love your children and that you are proud of their effort, persistence, and continued improvement. Of course also remember there is such a thing as, too much failure and that girls should not just go through the motions during activities. Our daughter need to have some success in order to bolster motivation, build confidence, reinforce effort, and increase enjoyment. Bottom line as our daughters pursue their life goals, they must experience a healthy balance of success and failure to gain the most from their efforts.

Teach your daughter that her body is her own & that she has a right to say "no"

Part of raising strong, independent, and self-confident daughters is teaching them that they- and they alone- have full control over their own bodies. In an ideal world, no one would ever touch anyone else's body without that person's full consent. Things like assault and abuse wouldn't exist. Sadly, that's not the world we live in. In fact, in many parts of our great country it's only getting worse. We need to teach our kids- both our boys and our girls- that their body belongs to them. Part of that starts early by not forcing kids to give hugs against their will.

As they get older, when you have "the talk" with your daughter, reiterate that no one should ever, ever, ever force her to do something that she doesn't want. It doesn't matter what she's wearing or what her date expects, she's always allowed to say no.

Just as important, make sure she knows that she can come to you if someone doesn't accept "no" for an answer and that you will not punish her for anything that she did prior to the assault. According to a 2018 Study by Kanas State University, too many of our teenage daughters are afraid to tell their parents about an assault because they're afraid of repercussions. For example, a teen that snuck out to go to a party may be afraid to tell her parents that a boy at the party assaulted her because she doesn't want to get in trouble for sneaking out. We as parents must make sure our girls know that no matter the situation they can come to us with no questions asked, Period.

Final Thoughts

Strong girls know that her body is her own and that if anyone does not respect her that the people who love her will make damn sure that it doesn't happen again and proper consequences occur.

CHAPTER 5

MAY

"Strong women don't have 'attitudes', we have standards." –Marilyn Monroe

Strong girls do not make the same mistakes over and over again

It's easy for our daughters to get frustrated and self-critical when they repeat mistakes. We as parents need to first make sure that they understand that they are not the only one who does this. Second, we need to teach the girls in our life how to correct their actions so they can become truly strong. Remember that just vowing to never make a particular mistake again is the wrong approach. We need to teach the females in our live how to first identifies the mistake that is being made and then how to take the proper steps to not make the same mistake over and over again.

Identify the mistake that is being made

The key to solving any problem is to understand what the problem is in the first place. You and your daughter must take some time to think about a mistake she made or a recent failure and maybe write it at the top of a piece of paper so there is a visual reminder.

Identify what a successful resolution will look like.

The next step to take is to identify what a successful resolution will look like. On the sheet of paper, have your daughter write out what she feels would quantify as a successful resolution. What is it that she is working toward? What is your goal? What are you aiming to achieve? Have her write that down, but understand that success may not look exactly as she may envision, so make sure she doesn't get too wrapped up in the idea of what this success will be.

Things may change. She may eventually find that her standards for success were off because of a lack of knowledge or experience about the thing.

Trace the route of your decision making that brought you to making the same mistake.

At this point, it is time to reverse-engineer the route that brought her to making the same mistake over and over. She does this by asking questions. Questions such as: (please note these questions are for older girls and need to be modified for age.)

- Did I lack knowledge? Information? Experience? Perspective?
- Is there a point where I could have made different decisions that would have brought me to not making this mistake?
- What role did I play in this mistake?
- What factors negatively impacted me causing me to make the same mistake over and over?

Develop a strategy and course of action to reach your successful resolution.

It's time to develop a strategy. Help your daughter figure out what elements are going to bring her to a successful resolution. What pitfalls does she need to avoid? What steps need to be taken to insure the same mistake is never made again? We must help our daughters map these steps out on your sheet of paper. Remember to make this age appropriate and mistake appropriate. Some mistakes are larger and harder to fix then others.

Be willing to try again with your new and different strategy.

The most important step of pursuing success is to be willing to accept failure and try again. Your daughter's new plan might not work out. That's just how it goes sometimes. Depending on what you and your daughter tried, you may need to change your strategy and try again.

The upside is that you gain a fair amount of experience as you work through this process. The downside, of course, is that no one likes to feel like they are failing or not making due progress.

The only real strategy is to grin and bear it, keep pushing forward, adjust your strategy, but don't lose your goal in the process. You can overcome and succeed!

Final thoughts

Our daughters cannot completely eliminate all mistakes from their life. However they can aim to improve their standard of living by not making the same mistake over and over again. Once they stop repeating the same mistakes (Sasha) only then can they become truly strong!

Help her identify family values

Family values have the power to shape and strengthen not only the daughters but everyone from mom and dad to your neighbors and the people who comes in contact with on a daily basis. Once your daughter takes ownership of those values, she can help shape them to be in line with what she envisions your family to be.

Let's define family values, why they're important, and how they can be instilled into your daughter's daily life starting ASAP.

What are family values?

Family values are similar to personal values or work values, but they include the entire family. Regardless of what your family looks like, how many parents and children it may (or may not include), these values inform family life and how you deal with challenges as a unit.

They also establish the value system under which children grow up and everyone (old and young) mature and develop as individuals. Family values can guide your entire family to become the kind of people you want to be. And ultimately, if your family includes children, family values can have a huge influence on child-rearing.

Why family values are important

Whenever someone in your family goes through a teachable moment, your family values will shine through. This is true whether those values are intentional or not.

Here's how family values contribute to your loved ones and relationships.

1. They guide family decisions

Family values define what you and the other people in your family consider being right or wrong. These values can help you stay consistent when making decisions in everyday life. They can also guide those decisions in moments of uncertainty.

This is especially true when you're tempted to make rash decisions based on an emotional reaction. When you have clearly established family values, you can take a step back. Instead of acting impulsively, what do your values suggest is the right course of action?

For instance, how do you deal with someone who has lied to another family member? How do you set boundaries with your middle school daughter who wants to go a high school party and with younger girls when is their bedtime?

2. They provide clarity and structure

Remember that girls learn by modeling what the people around them do. Because of the plasticity of their brains, they can adapt and change depending on what environment they grow up in.

When their parents or guardians follow a set of clear values, they have clarity on what is right and wrong. Values give them structure and boundaries within which they can thrive.

On the other hand, unclear values can create inconsistencies for our daughters. They may struggle to figure out right from wrong if their family values constantly change.

And while you may have clear personal values, other adults in the family may have completely different values. When those values clash, it can be confusing for the girls involved.

Defining your family values helps avoid confusion and creates a clear definition of right and wrong.

3. They help your family achieve a sense of identity

Growing up is difficult! Girls are constantly trying to figure out who they are and who they want to be. And because their brains aren't fully developed yet, this process can be grueling on its own.

When you add in the other challenges that life can throw at them, you can imagine how hard it is to grow up.

Clear family values can help children build a sense of identity.

While the rest of the world around them is uncertain, they know they can rely on their family values to identify themselves.

Family values can also give the family its own sense of identity as a family unit.

4. They improve communication among family members

When values are clear, communication is easier. Everyone is on the same page. All family members are working with the same definition of right and wrong.

It's much easier to have productive conversations when there isn't any ambiguity in values. This can help maintain a healthy family dynamic.

Types of family values

Most core values for families fall into specific categories.

Here are five types of family values that all families should establish. Not all families will have the same approach to these values, but defining them is important.

1. Relationship to others

Your family likely has a set of values that dictate how to behave around others. These values can also define how you develop relationships with other people.

You don't just have to define values for how you want to treat the people you have close relationships with. How do you and your family believe you should treat other people in general, including strangers?

Some families believe everyone deserves respect. Other families believe this respect needs to be earned first.

How your family views their relationships with others can also help you determine how to handle unpleasant situations. For instance, how would you deal with children in your family being bullied? Or, how would you react if children in your family bullied someone else?

And how do you treat relationships with your extended family?

These are all important questions to consider when establishing your family values.

2. Relationship with each other

In some cases, the way you handle family relationships will differ from how you handle outside relationships.

For instance, some families work under the assumption that family comes first, no matter what. Other families prefer a more egalitarian approach.

In either case, it's important to define values that determine how family members treat each other. These values can define:

- How children should act with each other
- How children should act toward their parents
- How spouses deal with their children (how child care is handled)
- How spouses treat each other
- How parents co-parent

3. Relationship to oneself

Family values can set rules for how to treat others, in and out of the family. But they can also guide how every person treats themselves.

How should individuals act when they've done something wrong? What should they do when they're having a bad day or having a hard time dealing with their emotions?

Values about how to treat oneself can often be forgotten or set aside. But how you treat yourself is just as important as the way you treat others.

4. Priorities

What does your family prioritize? Some values can define what matters to your family first and what's less important.

Some examples include:

- How you spend family time
- What spiritual or religious rituals matter to your family
- What type of education you'll provide for your children

- How you deal with holiday stress
- How you create traditions and celebrate different cultures
- Defining priorities can also guide your family when making tough decisions. For example, where will you make budget cuts when your family is under financial stress?

5. Dealing with challenges

Challenges are inevitable. No matter how much you prepare yourself and your family, you'll one day have to face hardships. Your values dictate how your family reacts and adapts when these challenges come your way.

Examples ma include:

- Resilience
- Perseverance
- Patience

When you establish these types of values, you'll give your family the tools they need to get through tough times.

8 family value examples

There are endless possibilities for a potential list of values you can instill in your family. In case you need a starting point, here are eight examples of modern family values.

Self-compassion

Self-compassion means you should be kind to yourself first. It also means you should avoid negative self-talk.

If this is one of your family values, it's important to teach everyone in your family how to be compassionate to themselves. By learning how to be kind to themselves, they'll also learn how to be compassionate toward others.

For example, clinical psychologist Chris Germer teaches people to use physical touch, like touching your hand, with a self-compassionate statement. You can say something like, "I'm going through a challenging time, but I'm trying my best."

Empathy and kindness toward others

Once the youth in your family learn how to be kind to themselves, they have a solid base to be kind and empathetic toward others.

When you implement this value, you can learn to see the world through other people's eyes. This can inform the way you treat others.

Responsibility

When responsibility is part of your moral values, those in your family prioritize taking responsibility for their own actions.

But learning responsibility is also an amazing way for younger family members to learn how to contribute to the household. They can grow into a specific role within the family.

For example, you can use a simplified RACI matrix to establish who's responsible for what. Then, everyone can take ownership of their responsibilities.

Honesty

Honesty is an important value that many adults like to uphold. However, not all adults practice honesty with children.

If you decide to implement honesty as a family value, it's important that everyone within your family upholds this value to everyone else, regardless of age. Children will learn by seeing what you do.

Integrity

Some people confuse integrity with honesty. However, they're not the same.

Integrity requires honesty. But it goes deeper than just being honest.

Someone with integrity is reliable and trustworthy. They also value openness. Plus, someone with integrity will usually be responsible and accountable for their own actions.

Having integrity means respecting yourself and others. It's also important to express gratitude when others help you. Conversely, you should help others who are in need, as long as you don't jeopardize your own health or safety by doing so.

Implementing and respecting boundaries

Everyone should be able to uphold their own boundaries. But not all families make it a point to set and prioritize those boundaries.

Families who value boundaries need to learn how to communicate effectively. That's because it's difficult to remind others of your boundaries when you're not sure how to communicate them.

If you have children, communicating boundaries is crucial to help them learn that they are allowed to say no. They'll also learn that they need to respect the boundaries of other people, too.

Family time

When family time is part of your values, making space for quality time together is a priority.

Everyone in a family will have other things going on in their lives. However, this value ensures that everyone sets aside the time to regroup and bond with each other.

Family time can happen monthly, weekly, or even daily. One way that you can prioritize family time is to implement at least one family meal a day where everyone is fully present. This could mean electronic devices are put away during the meal.

You can also establish recurring traditions. Examples include:

- A monthly outing to the park
- Weekly family meetings
- Annual apple picking in the fall

Perseverance

Teaching and prioritizing perseverance and hard work is a way to help your family not give up at the first signs of failure.

Perseverance helps to normalize failure. It helps children to accept that failure can be an important part of learning.

It also teaches them how to be patient when they don't immediately get the end result they were hoping for.

Perseverance is an important skill in nearly all aspects of life. At work, perseverance can help you get promoted. At home, it can give you the strength to keep going when personal projects fail.

However, it's important to teach children to respect their limits, too. Perseverance shouldn't come at the expense of well-being. Perseverance without self-care can lead to burnout.

Final thoughts

Family values are the roots of the next generation. They inform what kind of women our future decision-makers will grow up to become.

For example, if several families implement generosity in their values, the next generation will grow up to be more generous. As a result, adults in this generation are more likely to take other people's needs into consideration when making important decisions.

While younger generations are still growing up, they'll one day be the ones holding positions of power.

They'll also be the ones to rise the next generation of young people when they have their own families.

In that sense, family values are one of the most impactful components of society. Even if you don't yet see the connection, your family values are directly connected to how society will evolve and how your daughter will become truly strong!!

Teach your Daughter to get more sleep

Our girls need sleep, plain and simple. We all do. Without enough sleep, we get cranky and, with time, unhealthy. But for children, it's especially important because the effects of sleep deprivation can lead to lifelong problems.

Studies by the University of Michigan have shown that kids not getting enough sleep can contribute to obesity. But even more troubling, studies show that children who don't get enough sleep can end up with behavioral and learning problems that persist for years. Teens that don't get enough sleep are at higher risk for depression and learning problems, and once they are old enough for drivers licenses are more likely to get into car accidents. The bottom line is in order for our kids to be extraordinary they need more sleep.

Here are the recommended amounts of sleep per age group according to the National academy of sleep 2019 study of proper sleep habits:

- Infants: 12 to 16 hours (including naps)
- Toddlers: 11 to 14 hours (including naps)
- Preschoolers: 10 to 13 hours (including naps)
- Grade school-aged children: 9 to 12 hours
- Teens: 8 to 10 hours

Ultimately, though, it's up to us as parents to make sure their child gets enough sleep.

Here are four ways you can help your child get enough sleep:

Make sleep a priority

Parents must be sure to schedule time for sleep just like they do on a regular basis for homework, sports, and other activities. Start from when your child needs to get up in the morning, and then count back the number of hours your child needs to sleep and set a non-negotiable bedtime.

For tweens and teens, this may lead to some tough conversations and decisions about schedules and activities, and may mean cutting back on some activities, finding ways to get homework done earlier, and pushing some leisure activities (like video games) to weekends

Start the bedtime routine earlier.

Remember that it is really hard to go right from a physically or mentally intense activity right to sleep. If bedtime is 8:00 pm, that means that your child needs to start winding down between 7 and 7:30 so that they are ready to actually fall asleep at 8.

Shut off the screens.

A big part of winding down is making sure our kids shut off their screens; the blue light emitted from screens can wake up the brain and make it harder to fall asleep. This is particularly true for "small screens" such as phones or tablets that are held closer to the face. Shut them off an hour before you want your child to be asleep. Phones should be charged outside of the bedroom — or at the very least, put in Do Not Disturb mode. If your child tries to tell you they need their phone to wake them up in the morning, buy them an alarm clock.

Keep the same sleep routines on weekends

Another important way parents can be sure their child gets enough sleep is to try and keep the same sleep routines on the weekends. A little leeway is okay, like staying up an hour or so later if your child can and will sleep later in the morning (if you have one of those kids who is up at dawn no matter what aka my son Jaxson, staying up later may not work out so well).

Remember, the common theme of being a role model throughout this book, and that children pay more attention to what we as parents do than what we say. If you make your own sleep a priority, you will set a good example for your child — and feel better yourself.

Final thoughts

Parents remember that sleep is essential for the good health of our girls. In fact, just like food and water we need sleep to survive. We as parents need to make sure that our daughters are getting enough sleep so they don't experience side effects such as poor memory and focus, weakened immunity, and mood swings. Let's not overlook something that affects 1/3rd of our girl's life and make sure they are getting enough sleep daily. Once this occurs they will be one step closer to being truly strong girls!

CHAPTER 6

JUNE

"A strong women looks a challenge dead in the eye and gives it a wink" - Gina Carey

Strong Girls do not fear taking calculated risks.

We know from research that girls who take calculated risks, which learn to manipulate their environment and question their surroundings, are often demonstrated to be more resilient and capable as they mature. They are not afraid to take chances and pursue their goals. They welcome change and adapt well when things don't go as planned. They have that special 'bounce back' factor that allows them to pick themselves up, dust themselves off and carry on. These girls have been known to trust their "gut".

When it comes to taking risks, there's something to be said for trusting your gut. But too many people confuse a gut instinct with fear.

They assume their discomfort means their gut is telling them not to proceed. So rather than step outside their comfort zone, they avoid the risks that could propel them forward.

Our girls may not go out for a sport or apply for an afterschool job because they feel scared and that it might be too risky to put "themselves out there". We as parents must be able to insure them that are not an accurate way to measure risk and that they must overcome their fear.

Fear Causes You to Overestimate Risk

The bottom line is that the level of fear usually has nothing to do with the actual level of risk someone faces. Take, for example, public speaking. It's often cited as the No. 1 fear most people have. But public speaking isn't actually risky. Sure, there's some social risk involved-- people may judge your speaking ability or find your message boring. But their judgment won't kill you. Still, because public speaking feels risky, many people won't do it. On the other hand, most people don't think twice about jumping into a car and going for a drive. For the average person, that doesn't feel risky. Yet car crashes kill people every day. In fact, statistics show the odds of dying in a car accident over the course of your lifetime are 1 in 606. There's zero chance you'll die of stage fright from giving a speech.

The Absence of Fear Causes You to Underestimate Risk

When you have no fear at all--like when you're really excited about a new opportunity--there's a good chance you'll underestimate risk. Additionally, you'll overestimate your abilities and your chances of success.

That's why some people fall for get-rich-quick schemes. The promise of a giant return on their investment deludes them into thinking they're going to succeed. Because it doesn't feel scary, they assume it isn't risky.

Balance Emotion with Logic

We must teach our strong girls that their needs to be a balance and they cannot fear taking calculated risks. They must understand that taking the right risks could be the difference between living an ordinary life and living an extraordinary life.

But you can't calculate risk based on your level of fear. Instead, it's important to assess the actual level of risk by examining the facts. Create a list of the pros and cons and the potential risks versus benefits.

Writing down the facts and reading them over will help you view the risk with logic--and that's the key to balancing out your emotions.

When you're excited about an opportunity and know you're likely to overlook the risks, we must teach our girls to come to us so we can help them figure out "What are the potential drawbacks?" Talking about the downsides can help them become more rational.

On the flipside, when our daughters are too afraid to make a move, talk to someone about the potential benefits of moving forward. Hearing some words of wisdom from someone else may help them find the courage to take the leap.

Final Thoughts

To many girls these days shy away from breaking out of their comfort zones, mostly due to previous negative experiences when taking risks in the past; however, as parents we must quickly realizing that if our girls are going to be successful adults, they will need to learn to take smart risks in order to stand out from the crowd. Always remember that the biggest risk is not taking any risk. <u>Just imagine what greatness your daughter is capable of if they are allowed to believe that taking a risk can lead to winning – or learning – or changing the world.</u>

Teach her healthy eating from birth

One of the biggest challenges in raising girls is helping them develop a healthy body image, while avoiding the unhealthy eating habits that have led to a surge in childhood obesity. Like other things, there's no time that is too "early" to start. Below are lists of just a few eating strategies that can be applied at all ages.

Healthy eating strategies that work

- Serve appropriate portions
- Serve a balanced selection of healthy unprocessed whole foods.
- Don't keep unhealthy choices in the house
- Make sure your girls are getting all their proper vitamins and Minerals
- Let girls stop eating when they're no longer hungry (instead of insisting that they clear their plate).
- Involve your daughter in shopping, menu planning, and cooking.
- Eat together as a family as often as possible; make meal time family time.

Strategy 1: Serve appropriate portions

We have to remember that our daughters do not eat the same portions as our sons and that younger girls should not eat as much as their older sisters. However as portions have gotten bigger for adults, some parents and caregivers have developed a distorted view of the amount of food our daughter's needs. In many cases young girls have as much food on their plate as adults, which is simply way too much. The biggest mistake most parents make is thinking that their children is not eating enough and have kids eat more than they need. The result of parents giving children to large of portions or expect them to clean their plate is being overweight and obese. The United States is facing a health crisis related to obesity. An alarming statistic from the center for disease control and prevention 2017 study found that 22% of children starting school are either overweight or obese. One of the main reasons has been an increase portion sizes. A USDA (2016) children's health and wellness study found that some portion sizes are now double what they were 20 years ago.

According to the USDA dietary guidelines (2017), an appropriate serving size for children from the ages of 3 to 6 years of age is about one-half an adult serving. Younger girls need to consume about 1,000 to 1,200 calories per day. Here's how to distribute those calories in a healthy eating plan:

- Grain Group: About 3 to 4 ounces of grains per day, preferably half of them whole grains. For example, that is one or two slices of bread plus one cup ready-to-eat cereal and ½ cup cooked rice or pasta.
- Vegetable Group: 1 to 1½ cups raw or cooked vegetables per day. Like adults, young kids need variety: mashed sweet potatoes, broccoli with low-fat dip or tomato sauce for pasta.
- ·ruit Group: 1 cup fresh, frozen, canned, or dried per day. Limit juice to 4 to 6 ounces per day. Emphasize whole fruits rather than juice. Kids love melon balls, mandarin oranges (fresh or canned in juice) and frozen berries.
- Milk Group: 2 to 2½ cups per day. Whole milk is recommended for children younger than 2. Older children can have lower-fat, calcium-rich choices such as fat-free or low-fat milk, yogurt and cheese.
- Meat and Beans Group: 2 to 3 ounces total per day. Options include lean meat, poultry, fish, an egg, cooked beans (black, pinto, and kidney) and peanut butter.

One reason girls may not be eating appropriately sized portions are because parents and care givers may not recognize what a reasonable portion looks like. Many times in the past when giving seminars on nutrition people would ask, "What does one-half cup of rice look like? What about four ounces of chicken or two tablespoons of peanut butter? Instead of having to carry around measuring cups and scales it's easy to compare portion sizes to every day household items. An example of this would be one cup is the size of a baseball. Before serving your girls food or drink, you can think of the relevant object and choose a portion that matches its size.

Parents remember that food amounts given to your daughter should fall into the recommended ranges rather than specific amounts since young children have fluctuating appetites and tend to eat more at some meals and less at others. Parents can use the portion sizes as a guide on how much to offer to their young children, however they should then allow their daughter to eat to their appetite. Keep in mind that taller or more active children will eat larger portions than shorter or less active children. Parents must not urge young children to finish everything on the plate or to eat more than they want too.

Note: The amount of food and number of servings children need daily from each food group depends on their age and how active they are. Some parents worry because young children seem to eat small amounts of food, especially when compared with adult portions. Remember a child who is growing well is getting enough to eat. If you are concerned, talk with your child's doctor.

Strategy 2: Serve a balanced selection of healthy unprocessed whole foods.

A girls eating plan should consist mostly of healthy foods with a balance of protein, carbohydrates and healthy fats. A recommendation according to the USDA for each one of these nutrients is 40 % of carbohydrates, 30% protein and no more than 13% from fat. Here is an at-a-glance guide to the main food types which should be included in your child's diet

Carbohydrates

This group should make up the largest part (around 40 %) of your child's diet. Bread, rice, fruits and vegetables are the body's main source of energy and also provide vitamins, minerals and fiber. Carbohydrates are also a good source of iron which is essential for forming red blood cells which carry oxygen around the body. A good intake of iron is also necessary for energy, intellectual performance and vitality.

Try to choose wholegrain carbohydrates such as brown rice or bread, rather than white bread or rice. These foods release sugar relatively slowly into the bloodstream which helps provide long lasting energy. Also, refined carbohydrates like white bread have lost many of their valuable nutrients during processing.

Fruit and vegetable are also an important part of carbohydrates as they provide vitamins and minerals, which help protect against cancer and heart disease. Root vegetables in particular are an important carbohydrate for energy.

Recommended daily intake: School aged girls should eat about four servings of grain based carbohydrates each day. One serving is one slice of bread, a small portion of brown rice or pasta, or a small bowl of cereal. Children should also eat four to five servings of carbs in the form of fruits and vegetables. This could include half an apple, four dried apricots, a tablespoon of peas and one tomato.

Protein

Protein is very important for preschoolers since it is one of the most important for the growth, maintenance and repair of body tissue. Red meat provides the best and most easily absorbed source of iron as well, which is something that most girls do not get enough of. Also not enough protein can lower resistance to infection.

Younger girl's main source of protein comes from Dairy. Dairy foods provide not only protein but also vitamins and minerals and are the best source of calcium. Calcium is very important for bone and teeth health of young children.

Recommended daily intake: Girls should eat meat or chicken three to four times a week. Protein foods like cheese or eggs are a good source for breakfast: Children should have three portions of milk or dairy products each day. This could be a glass of milk, a cup of yoghurt, or a few pieces of cheese.

Fats

Healthy fats should make up twenty to thirty percent of a girls diet. Healthy fats come in the form of fish, milk, nuts and seeds and are critical for brain development and visual development. Including healthy fats in a girl's diet may help to improve the performance of children with learning difficulties as well.

Recommended daily intake: Your daughter should eat healthy fats three to four times a week.

Examples of healthy foods that every Girl should eat

Eggs offer protein, and they're one of the few foods that naturally contain vitamin D, which helps the body absorb calcium. Eating protein at breakfast helps kids feel satisfied longer.

Yogurt gives preschoolers plenty of good bacteria, also known as probiotics, which is key to keeping little stomachs happy and healthy. Be sure to limit sugary versions aimed at kids because these are often lower in protein and good bacteria. Instead, choose plain nonfat or low-fat yogurt or Greek yogurt. Look for the words "live and active cultures" on the carton to ensure that the yogurt has plenty of beneficial bacteria.

Flaxseed is a nutty plant food which is packed full of Omega-3 fatty acids. Omega-3 is needed for optimal brain development. Flaxseed is sold whole and ground, but research suggests that ground is absorbed by the body better. Try sprinkling ground flaxseed onto cereal or into the batter of pancakes or waffles. Replace 1/4 cup of flour with ground flaxseed in your child's favorite muffin, bread, or cupcake recipe to add a healthy boost to baked goods.

Sweet Potato is one of the most nutritious (and inexpensive) vegetables around. The Vitamin A in sweet potatoes keeps eyes healthy, and acts like an antioxidant in the body. Sweet potatoes are a favorite among preschool because of their natural sweetness and bright color, but they are often forgotten once kids get older. Try a baked sweet potato the next time you need a side dish. Simply wash, pierce with a fork, and bake at 375 degrees for 45 minutes or until tender.

Black Beans are a great source of protein, as well as fiber and calcium—two things kids tend not to get enough of. The best ways to get preschoolers to eat these beans is by Making nachos or quesadillas with black beans, cheese and salsa.

Mango is a sweet tropical fruit that will provide your daughter with almost a whole day's supply of Vitamin C in just one fruit. The vitamin C helps keep kids' immune systems running strong and keeps teeth and gums healthy. It also provides 3 grams of fiber for just around 100 calories. Buy fresh or jarred in juice to serve cut up or in a smoothie or dessert like Banana-Mango Smoothie or Double Mango Pudding.

Blueberries rank among the healthiest fruits for years. Now research suggests that in addition to protecting against heart disease and diabetes and improving brain function. Another fruit that is great for your girl is **cantaloupe**, which provides vitamin C, beta-carotene, bits and pieces of B vitamins and trace minerals and calcium. Melons are not to be missed when they're plentiful and in season.

Overall the same healthy foods that adults eat preschoolers should eat as well. The key is to expose young children to a variety of healthy food choices and then let the child decide what foods they enjoy eating.

Strategy 3: Don't keep unhealthy food choices in the house

The food choices parents have been making for their daughters have become alarming. A study done by the Mayo clinic (2016) found that young children now more than any other time in history are consuming too much sodium, saturated fat, and sugar. According to a 2017 FDA study on the eating habits of preschoolers found about 85% of girls consumed a sweetened beverage, a dessert, or a sweet or salty snack three or more times a day !

Foods such as soda, chips, French fries, candy and fast food are high in salt, saturated fat and sugar, and low in nutrients. Many of these foods also contain bad fats that can increase the risk of childhood obesity and conditions like type-2 diabetes.

Foods that Girls should avoid Soda

This one should be a no-brainer, since hundreds of studies link soda and other sugar-sweetened beverages to obesity, type 2 diabetes, and aggressive behavior in children. Research by Addessi E, Galloway AT, Visalberghi E, and Birch LL (2005) found that a vast majority of American kids are still chugging these drinks. A 20-ounce bottle of soda can have over 60 grams of sugar. Some of these drinks have four times what kids should get in an entire day. According to Joan Blake (2016), Children just don't have much room in their diets for beverages that supply a ton of empty calories and no nutrients. Many soda also have caffeine which children should not have due to the fact caffeine stops the body from absorbing calcium well and can lead to stunted growth.

Microwave popcorn

Up until about three years ago, I had never even heard of perfluorooctanoic acid, or PFOA. It's the chemical used to line the bags of microwave popcorn so that they don't catch on fire. Many studies, Including ones by the FDA, The Mayo Clinic and Ohio State University show that PFOA has been linked to cancer, postponed puberty, thyroid disease and high cholesterol in kids. Microwave popcorn is also full of sodium and saturated fat from imitation butter flavor which is so often found on microwave popcorn. The best alternative is to just pop your own popcorn over the oven or in a popcorn machine.

Processed meats

Meats such as Hot dogs, bologna, and other packaged lunch meat may sound like kid-friendly foods, but they are loaded with fat, nitrates, sodium and preservatives which can all be harmful to your preschooler's development. These foods have also been found to increase a kid's risk of heart disease, diabetes and colon cancer. If your child loves lunch meats, opt for preservative-free varieties whenever possible.

Cereal

There is no aisle more attractive to preschoolers than the cereal aisle. "With its rainbow of colors and variety of cartoon characters, sugary kid's cereals are probably some of the most begged for foods in the supermarket."(Havermans RC and Jansen A. (2007) Parents remember that rainbow colored bits of oats or rice is not healthy, and no amount of sprayed on vitamins or extra fiber will make them so. In a recent analysis, Consumer Reports (2016) found that only two (cheerios and kixs) out of 50 kinds of cereal were low enough in sugar and high enough in fiber to be considered good foods for kids.

Boxed mac and cheese

Boxed mac and cheese is highly processed and has little to any nutrients due to the fact it's loaded with sodium and preservatives. The better alternative is to make mac and cheese from scratch, which is simple just be sure to buy whole-grain pasta, fresh cheese, and any other fresh not processed ingredients that you and your kids would like to add.

Fruit Snacks

Gummy fruit snacks, and fruit rolls are all sugar with no real fruit. Parents should view fruit snacks like candy instead of a nutritional snack. Even though today in many grocery stores fruit snacks now say "made with real fruit" or "made with real fruit juice," this still does not make them healthy. Most fruit snacks are still packed with as much sugar as a can of soda. If you're looking for an easy snack with some actual nutrition, go with dried real fruit instead.

Crackers

Most parents have some crackers packed away incase their preschooler gets hungry and you're in public with no restaurants in sight. Though they might quiet down a cranky hungry little one, crackers have little nutrients since they are made of processed white flour, preservatives, and unhealthy oils. A better alternative is air popcorn or whole grain crackers that do not use white flour.

Avoid Trans-fat at all cost

The worse possible foods girls can eat are Tran's fats. Tran's fat was developed as a substitute for butter; food manufacturers put vegetable oils through a process called *hydrogenation*. The addition of hydrogen makes the product firm and resistant to spoilage. However, while hydrogenated or Trans fats spread like butter, they also share some of the unwanted properties of saturated fats. They appear to interfere with removing LDL ("bad") cholesterol from the blood and also lower HDL ("good") cholesterol. As a result, foods with trans-fat greatly contribute to obesity, heart disease and certain cancers. Tran's fats can be found in many foods preschoolers enjoy such as fried foods like doughnuts, and baked goods including cakes, pie crusts, biscuits, frozen pizza, cookies, crackers, and stick margarines and other spreads. Parents can determine the amount of Tran's fats in a particular packaged food by looking at the Nutrition Facts panel. Tran's fat is the one food that parents should try to avoid and try to totally cut out of their child's diet.

Strategy 4: Make sure Girls are getting all their proper Vitamins and Minerals

In today's society many parents do not have the time to cook their daughter nutritious, well balanced meals and opt for fast food. Most of these convenience meals are full of processed food with little nutritional values. Because of this many pediatricians recommend a daily multivitamin or mineral supplement. I recommend that all parents of girls talk to their child's doctor and get their expert opinion on if they need vitamins, minerals or maybe another type of food supplement. Your family doctor will be able to give you the proper dose and recommend the proper brands for your child.

Traditionally medical professionals recommend girls that aren't eating enough food throughout the day or like stated before are eating a lot of fast food and processed food should take a vitamin supplement. Girls who do not eat a lot of meat or have a dairy free diet may need supplements to meet the recommends of iron and calcium as well.

Here is a list of the Top Six Vitamins and Minerals that your daughter could supplement in her diet.

- Vitamin A promotes normal growth and development; tissue and bone repair; and healthy skin, eyes, and immune responses. Good sources include milk, cheese, eggs, and yellow-to-orange vegetables like carrots, yams, and squash.
- Vitamin B. The family of B vitamins -- B2, B3, B6, and B12 -- aid metabolism, energy production, and healthy circulatory and nervous systems. Good sources include meat, chicken, fish, nuts, eggs, milk, cheese, beans, and soybeans.
- Vitamin C promotes healthy muscles, connective tissue, and skin. Good sources include citrus fruit, strawberries, kiwi, tomatoes, and green vegetables like broccoli.
- Vitamin D promotes bone and tooth formation and helps the body absorb calcium. Good sources include milk and fatty fish like salmon and mackerel. The best source of vitamin D is sunlight.

- Calcium helps build strong bones as a child grows. Good sources include milk, cheese, yogurt, tofu, and calcium-fortified orange juice.
- Iron builds muscle and is essential to healthy red blood cells. Iron deficiency is a risk in adolescence, especially for girls once they begin to menstruate. Good sources include beef and other red meats, turkey, pork, spinach, beans, and prunes.

If your daughter is taking vitamins or other supplements make sure they are well out of reach of children since most taste good and children could easily mistake as candy. Remember that large doses of vitamins aren't a good idea for children. The fat-soluble vitamins (vitamins A, D, E, and K) can be toxic if kids overdose on excessive amounts. The same goes for iron as well. Your daughter *can* get too much of a good thing.

Always remember that fresh food is the best source of vitamins and should be the first choice for our girls over giving them nutrients in pill form. After all healthy preschoolers get their best start from what you put in your grocery cart not in the medicine cabinet.

Strategy 5: Let Girls stop eating when they're no longer hungry (instead of insisting that they clear their plate).

A study published in the journal <u>Pediatrics (2016)</u> found half of all parents expect their adolescent children to clean their plates, while a third prompted them to eat more - even after they stated they were full. There's no reason for parents to provide pressure for girls with normal development and health to clean their plate!

Research suggests when parents make children clean their plate; they can lose their ability to follow their own hunger cues and to stop eating when they're full. According to a study by Mayo Clinic in 2016, Overtime, children forced to clean their plates at every meal may gravitate toward sugary foods and snacks and run the risk of becoming overweight or obese.

In a recent survey, some daycare workers mistakenly believed a clean plate club approach would encourage kids to develop a healthy appetite, researchers report in the Journal of the Academy of Nutrition and Dietetics (2017). This study also found that childcare providers use controlling feeding practices because of fear of parents' negative reaction if they find that their child did not eat. We as parents must make sure childcare providers, grandparents and anyone else who is in charge of feeding our children that it is ok if they choose not to eat or finish their food. Also we as parents must make sure childcare providers should avoid practices such as giving food as reward, and praising preschooler for cleaning their plates. Dr. Rowell, a childhood feeding specialist recommends having a conversation with the child-care provider or teacher. She also created a Lunchbox Card that parents can print, laminate, and put in your child's lunch box that asks teachers not to interfere at mealtime.

The good news is that when children are not forced to clean their plates they become healthier later in life. Researchers at the University of Minnesota (2016), for instance, have found that girls who were not forced to clean their plates grew up to be young adults who used the internal cues of hunger and fullness to guide their eating habits. These young adults who followed internal cues on hunger not only had a lower body mass index than those who used external cues, but they also had lowered instances of disordered eating.

Strategy 6: Involve Girls in menu planning, shopping, and cooking

The act of involving girls in the process of planning, shopping and cooking what they should eat is an important step in raising healthy eaters. The menu planning process can means sampling giving your child a choice of what healthy foods they would like to eat. An example of this could be having the child pick chicken or fish, brown rice or sweet potatoes, or carrots or beans. According to Amanda Nunez of the American Council for healthy eat, by allowing children to make choices they now can ownership over what they put into their body.

The second step in preschool involvement is going to the grocery store with them. The shopping trip should be an interactive experience where you as the parent points out the healthy foods your child can choose for the meals they are going to eat. During this time as a parent we can point out how to tell if fruits and vegetables are rip or not and what the best cuts of meat are. Remember this should be a time to talk about healthy food options not just a quick run through isles where the parent puts stuff in the cart then checks out quickly.

The third step in child food involvement is preparation and cooking. Have your girl perform age appropriate task such as washing the produce, measuring and dumping in ingredients and stirring and mixing. Once the food is prepared then allow for your child to watch as you bake, steam or cook the food. This part is usually not as age approaches, however with close supervision they should be allowed to watch the food cook.

Children who attend day care can apply the involvement method by having parents make a lists of what items you have available for different parts of their lunches and have them choose from the items when packing their lunch or snack. Your girl should know they need an entree item, at least one fruit, a vegetable, and a healthy snack. Cross items out when they are used or you run out and then repeat the choosing and shopping process.

Now, I'm not suggesting you give your girl gets executive control over grocery shopping and meal planning. Instead, I'm suggesting that you start with once a week and then move to two or three meals. Having kids involved in the meal planning and preparation process does take more time and effort but in the long run well worth the long term habits that will be learned and then passed down to other generations.

Final Thoughts

If girls learn to eat a variety of healthy foods and balanced meals from birth, they'll be much better positioned to avoid unhealthy habits, like developing an unhealthy body image, when they're older. Always remember that a healthy girl is a strong girl!

Have your girl play sports

Having your daughter participate in sports is another step that we as parents can take to make sure she grows up to become strong women. Youth sports promote the value and importance physical activities can have on the emotional, bodily, social, and mental development of your girl. Here are some other really good reasons why you should sign your daughter up for sports as soon as possible.

Social Skills

When playing sports kids will communicate and interact with other kids and adults (coaches). One of the most important traits children need to develop is their social skills. The best way to develop your child's social skills is by having them participate in sports. Especially in team sports, kids will have to communicate with coaches and teammates on a regular basis. Parents, the bottom line is if you want your kids to be more social you have to put them in social situations.

Physically Fitness

Childhood obesity is running rampant across our entire country. Obesity is contributed to poor dietary habits and constant inactivity. Playing sports will keep kids physically active. Sports will compel kids to become better athletes because they will be executing a variety of different exercises during practice. They will strengthen their body and the constant exercise will help reduce stress and build their self-esteem. Let's not forget that physical fitness will help develop coordination as well. Kids that play sports will have better balanced, core strength, posture, and overall coordination than a kid that sits and plays video games all day long. When parents allow their children to become obese, they are setting them up for failure.

Keeps Kids Busy

Sports will keep kids busy and around other kids that are on the same path. Participating in sports will put your child in a safe and structured environment. They will be learning a variety of different skills that they will take with them as they grow older. I much rather have my kid come home from school and go to practice, rather than come home and go on YouTube all night long. Also according to the Department of Education, kids that participate in sports on a regular basis are less likely to drop out of school and do drugs.

Develops Competitiveness

Life is full of situations where you have to compete. One of the worst traits you can have is the unwillingness to compete. In today's world if people aren't willing to compete they will find themselves getting the short end of the stick on a regular basis. Being competitive isn't just about being better than everyone else. Kids need to learn to challenge and compete with themselves to become better every day. Every single successful person I know is competitive. They are not just competing with others; they are very driven and are always competing with themselves. When kids grow older they will need to be competitive in school, for jobs, and in all aspects of life. Always remember to teach your kids that it's a competitive world out there.

Friendships

I've played team sports my entire life. To this day, I am still in contact with many of my former teammates. When you participate in sports you go through so much with your teammates. You practice and work hard together all year long. This creates a bond that no other activity can replicate. The bottom line is playing sports will develop relationships that could last a lifetime.

Taking Instruction = Better Grades

In order to be successful in life you will need to learn how to take instruction. Participating in sports will teach kids how to take orders from someone of authority. According to a study by U.C.L.A., when kids are receptive to instruction, they will be able to learn very quickly and they will be able to handle a heavy workload. Remember that sports just doesn't exercise your muscles, sports exercises your brain as well.

Winners and Losers

Playing sports will teach your kids how to win and how to lose. In the majority of sports competitive there will be a winner and a loser. Sometimes kids will be on the winning team and sometimes they will be on the losing team. Sports will teach kids how to come off a defeated and continue to work hard.

Conclusion

Parents remember that sports are a part of our culture and touch nearly everyone's life to some degree. Getting your daughter involved in sports has many benefits but this only happen is your kids are having fun. If you or your daughter is hesitant, take them to a game and let them see how the sports work and the interaction among the players. Soon they will be itching to join the fun and then becoming extraordinary will soon follow.

CHAPTER 7

JULY

"Above all, be the heroine of your life, not the victim". – Nora Ephron

Strong girls do not think the world owes them anything

Sad to say that our daughters can be the wrecking balls of their own lives. They alone can stand in the way of personal freedom and peace of mind, all because of their own selfish expectations and desires. Too many people are going about their daily lives as if the world owes them something that somehow privilege is their birthright and they are superior to all. When in fact, no, the world owes nobody anything and this illusion destroys and separates, the oneness of humanity and steals the true meaning and magic of life.

We must teach our daughters to be a responsible person. If they want something – whether it's happiness, wealth, power, success or <u>love</u> – you need to WORK for it yourself.

<u>Life doesn't owe you anything: not perfect parents or a perfect childhood, not even immunity from pain or problems, a house, a bed, a job or even a single meal.</u>

If she haven't sweated or struggled for something, why should she think she deserves it?

Once your girl realizes the truth – that the world doesn't owe her anything – she can start to create her own happiness. It is a GIFT to yourself when you acknowledge, accept and realize everything you DO have in your life needs to be earned.

This planet was free from civilization for an infinitely long time. Take a look outside; do you really think it was all just made for you? Do you really think the universe cares about your shiny new car or your fancy cell phone or whether you get the job you want? Sorry to inform you, but life isn't bothered with your artificial sense of value and importance in terms of your role here on planet earth. P.S. what truly matters is how you treat others around you. Are you a good friend? A good parent? A good spouse? These are what truly matter in this world. When the girls in our lives figure this out then they will be truly strong!

Teach your girl to Aim for Excellence

Does your daughter seem contented just coasting through life? Are they doing just enough to get by, while never making the most of their potential? Most parents do not want their daughters to grow up living in their basement watching tiktok videos all day. So it is of the upmost importance we as parents teach our girls to see the significance of aiming for excellence.

Just to be clear, aiming for "excellence" is not merely referring to getting straight A's or racking up accomplishments on the basketball court. There's nothing wrong with working towards these kinds of achievements. But the pursuit of excellence is about much more than that. It's about the following:

- Becoming the best that you can be.
- Cultivating a deep love for learning.
- Making a difference in the lives of others.
- Maximizing your talents and abilities.

This section will give you as parent's ways to inspire your children to pursue excellence.

Emphasize contribution over achievement

Many children and teens lose motivation when they feel as though they can't live up to the expectations of those around them. This applies especially in the area of academics, because they feel strong pressure to achieve certain grades. When they don't get those grades, they become discouraged. To enable your children to regain focus and motivation, emphasize that education isn't primarily about getting good grades. Instead, it's about acquiring the skills and knowledge that will allow them to contribute more effectively. By focusing on contribution rather than achievement, your children will find greater purpose in their education. This will make it more likely that they'll pursue excellence.

Show your daughter that hard work is enjoyable

In order for your daughter to make the most of their potential, they'll need to put in plenty of hard work. The problem is most of our children see hard work as something to be avoided whenever possible. But hard work is both meaningful and rewarding. To help your children see this, share with them the joy of overcoming obstacles, solving problems, and reaping the fruit of their labor. Gradually, they'll start to see that hard work isn't something to be dreaded. It's something to be enjoyed!

Give your daughter descriptive praise

What's descriptive praise? It's the kind of praise where you acknowledge your children's good behavior by specifically describing what they did, rather than using generic phrases like "Well done" or "Good job".

For example, you might say to your children, "I noticed that you finished all your homework before going out with your friends. That's very responsible of you."

Descriptive praise is an effective tool in encouraging your children to improve their attitude and effort which will lead to excellence.

Focus on solutions – not problems

This is especially important when it comes to parents own life, because after your entire attitude affects your children's attitude.

So make an effort to reframe problems as opportunities, and explain to your children how you're taking advantage of these opportunities. By doing so, they'll be more likely to embrace this positive mindset too.

In addition, teach your children to ask this question whenever they're faced with a difficult situation: "What is one thing I can do right now to make the situation better?" This is a powerful question that will open their eyes to the productive actions they could take, rather than indulging in complaining.

Conclusion

As a parent, you want your daughter to maximize their potential, and to find long-term fulfillment and success. In order for this to happen we must do what we can for our girls to aim for excellence. When this occurs our girls will be one step closer to be truly strong!

Teach your girl to be Good Listeners

Attention all parents; we need to recognize that good listening skills are essential to learning. In fact, according to James Oakland a Children Development specialist at the University of Washington, children who listen well not only develop strong language abilities, they find gaining knowledge in any subject easier, less stressful and more successful. After all attentive listeners retain most of what they hear in the classroom which translated to less time studying and better grades.

The typical baby is a born listener. In fact, according to Dr. Graham from Mayo Clinic, newborn baby's auditory system is the most strongly developed of all the sensory systems. Hearing may be slightly impeded by fluid in the baby's inner ear, but in baby's eagerness to engage they will work around that. Infants tune in to their parents' voices from the womb and are highly motivated to continue doing so. Their survival depends on the ability to listen and learn to communicate needs. The big question is what happens between birth and going to school. The answer is unclear, but here are some ways parents can ensure the development of amazing listening skills for their strong girls.

Remove or avoid distractions.

When we teach our girls to be good listens we must teach them to take a moment to anticipate possible distractions and remove them. Our girls need to make sure their cell phones are turned off first and foremost, also they need to make sure that TV, radio, or any other device that could be distracting are off.

If your daughter is in a social setting, and they are speaking one-on-one with someone, teach them to try to step aside to a quiet space where they won't be pulled away or interrupted by other people. Definitely teach them not to look over the other person's shoulder while they're talking to see who else is in the room.

Notice non-verbal communication and tone of voice.

According to Dr. M. L. Banks, the communications director of Harvard University, hearing someone's words is just a small part of being a good listener. We communicate far more through our expressions, body language, and tone of voice.

When you are listening to someone, also watch them carefully. Some examples of what to be aware of are as followed:

- Are their arms crossed defensively, or are they sitting in an open, confident manner?
- Are they saying, "Everything's fine" with their words, but their face looks pinched and anxious?

Also, listen to how they present what they have to say.

- Do they sound tired, depressed, enthusiastic, confused?
- Are they mumbling, talking too loudly, or stating everything as though it were a question?

As a listener we need to also make sure the following cues occur:

- Nod in agreement to show you are engaged and listening.
- Lean forward toward the other person.
- Smile or show concern appropriately.
- Offer words of affirmation and kindness.
- Give a hand squeeze or a warm touch on the shoulder to show empathy.

These subtle communications speak volumes about your level of engagement, understanding, and interest.

Don't interrupt or change the subject.

If you want your daughter to be a good listener, make sure to teach them to allow the speaker to complete a thought without interrupting them.

You've probably encountered people who frequently interrupt, take over the conversation, and use the audience as a platform for talking about themselves or sharing their knowledge or expertise and you probably found it very annoying. Let's raise extraordinary kids not annoying ones, there are already enough of them around.

Conclusion

Becoming a good listener is a skill that needs to be learned and must be practiced. It's far too easy to spin off into your own world of distractions, ideas, and words. As our daughters become more skilled at listening, they will find people gravitate toward them more. We as parents will be making sure our girls have a skill that gives them the edge in their future careers and in all of their future relationships.

CHAPTER 8

AUGUST

"Strong women don't play the victim. Don't make themselves look pitiful and don't point fingers. They stand and they deal." — Mandy Hale

Strong girls do not dwell on the past

Dwelling on the past means reading the same chapter over and over again while expecting the ending to change. Its reopening wounds and allowing opportunities for self-sabotage. So in order to raise strong daughters we must teach them that doing so is the biggest roadblock from moving forward, and bottom line is that life will move forward whether they are on board with it or not.

When they begin to recognize that it's time to move on, then they are letting the universe know that they are ready to accept and welcome change. Change is nothing to be scared about, because without change, there is no flow.

Here's a few ways that we can teach the girls in our lives how to stop dwelling on from the past and move on for good.

Remember You Are the Author of Your Own Story -Sasha

As a writer it is easy for me to use this metaphor; however we as parents need to make sure our daughters know that they alone are the author of their own book; this book is their whole life, and they are writing it as we speak. In this book, there are chapters, and each chapter tells the story of that particular year. For example, chapter 14 is a chapter that tells the tale of when you were 14-years-old, and chapter 30 is when you were thirty-years-old. Like a novel, each chapter introduces a series of supporting characters and events that will shake up your world. These supporting characters come in the form of friends, lovers, colleagues, and family members, all who are here to help the growth of the protagonist.

Now take a look at this book and see which chapter you are currently dwelling on. How many chapters have you written since then? How many chapters have you written before that? Now, how many times have you dwelled on the same chapter expecting the ending to change?

We have the power to write the ending to whatever we please, but we must keep writing our story. No one else will write it and can write it for you. Always remember that.

Own Your Mistakes and Grow from Them

The true art of letting go is ownership. This includes owning up to the mistakes you have made, acknowledging the imperfections we all have as humans, and opening yourself to grow from them.

It may be a tough pill to swallow, but studies show that forgiveness can lead to lower stress and anxiety levels. Forgiveness is a powerful tool for your daughter's self-growth and one of the most beneficial tools to prevent her from dwelling on the past.

You Can Only Connect the Dots Going Backward

In life, there will be moments when we realize that things had to unfold the way that they did. We will begin to understand why certain things didn't work in our favor, but connection will become clear in due time.

When our daughters dwell on the past this means resisting what's in store for them in the future. They must trust the process and give themselves some credit for coming this far.

Better Things Await

Our energy may be finite, but the possibilities of what we can achieve in this lifetime are infinite. Our daughters need to remember that they are using energy when dwelling on the past, when they worry, or when they become angry. Bottom line is that it's exhausting focusing on things that are out of your control.

Letting go is easier said than done, but like the muscles in our human body, this takes time to build and trust. Always remember that the beautiful thing about letting go is that you are making room for new things in your life.

Final Thoughts

We must always insure that our daughters understand that their past is only a single part of them and by no means the definition of who they are as a whole. They are currently evolving, learning, and nourishing themselves to be the best version they can be. Our girls must learn from the past, but never live there! When they realize this then they will become truly strong.

We must teach our daughters to Pray

We teach our daughter at a young age the colors of the world and how to count their fingers and toes. We teach them how to say "thank you" when they should be grateful and "I'm sorry" if they have made a mistake. We teach our daughters how to communicate what they are thinking and feeling. It is important that we teach them how to talk to others and it is even more crucial that we teach them how to talk with God. Parents need to pray with their daughter, but are we teaching them to pray on their own? Here are a few reasons why we as parents must take the time and teach our daughters how to pray:

1. **They will learn that God is real, and that he is God.** Jesus taught his disciples to pray saying, *"Our Father in heaven, hallowed be your name, your kingdom come, your will be done, on earth as it is in heaven" (Matthew 6:9-10).* When we teach our daughters to pray, we teach them to talk to the Creator of the world who is listening in heaven. When we honor God's name, we honor God as our all mighty. When children pray, they will understand that they have access to the God of the universe and God wants to talk with them. God wants to be their all mighty.

2. **Prayer is the way they will develop a close, personal relationship with God.** *"Be still, and know that I am God; I will be exalted among the nations, I will be exalted in the earth" (Psalm 46:10).* The strongest relationships in our lives are with people we have chosen to spend time with in a quiet, exclusive way. The same is true of our relationship with God. If the only time your daughter spends with God is also with other people, then God is most likely going to remain an "acquaintance" rather than a close, personal friend. Teach your daughter to be still and to spend time alone with God.

3. **They will learn that God loves them and listens to their prayers.** Jesus said, *"I will do whatever you ask in my name, so that the Father may be glorified in the Son. You may ask me for anything in my name,*

and I will do it" (John 14:13-14). It is normal for children to pray for everything they want, and to expect God to do whatever they ask of him. Most parents struggle with helping their child understand that God's answers to prayer are not always the same as their requests. Jesus said, "If you ask anything in my name, I will do it." He said, when you ask for what his holy and perfect character wants to give or does, he will do it. When our daughters pray they will learn that God loves them too much to give them something that is not perfect. They will also see their prayers answered, just as they asked. God loves to show his children that he loves them and listens to them. When our daughters pray, they will see God answer and know he heard their prayers.

4. **Children will learn that God's answers are unique and important.** *"Call to me and I will answer you and tell you great and unsearchable things you do not know" (Jeremiah 33:3)*. Children will often ask parents or friends for advice. One of the most important things our daughters can learn is that the only perfect advice is God's. God's answers are unique wisdom that can only be gained by "calling on the all mighty savor." One of the reasons parents need to teach their daughters to pray, is so that their girls will learn to turn to God for the answers that are "hidden" and that cannot be "known" any other way. That is a lesson that will carry them through life. (And it can make the high school and college years a little less stressful for parents!)

5. **Prayer will teach your daughter that when they make a mistake, there is help and forgiveness available to them, to make it right. (SASHA)** *"If we confess our sins, he is faithful and just and will forgive us our sins and purify us from all unrighteousness" (1 John 1:9)*. Prayer will help your daughter understand God's will for their lives, and that nobody makes perfect choices. Prayer is the first and best response when your daughter needs discipline. Prayer teaches them that God knows their failure and has a plan to redeem. (Sasha) When a parent prays with their child and asks God for wisdom

to know how to discipline, the child is much more likely to learn from that discipline. Your daughter will learn that they need to make their mistakes right with God and right with others (Sasha)!! Prayer will show your daughter that there is both consequence and forgiveness for mistakes and teach them that God redeems for his greater purpose (Romans 8:28).

Final thoughts

There is incredible power and potential in prayer. Through prayer, we invite the God of the Universe into a situation and into our lives. Prayer changes things, but even more prayer changes us. Through prayer, we have the opportunity to reach our full potential in Christ. The disciples said to Jesus, "Lord, teach us to pray." As we grow in our prayer life, we become more alive and more engaged with what God is doing. None of us are perfect at prayer, but as we take steps to grow spiritually in our prayer life, the impact is incredible. God will move mountains and God will transform us into people of love, joy, and peace through prayer. Let's become people of prayer and a church of prayer together. Through Prayer our daughters will become truly strong!!!!

Strong girls should always carry a pocket knife

Carrying a knife has been a time-honored tradition for throughout history. The Romans' invention of the folding pocket knife was a significant technological innovation in its day, making a knife safer to carry and easier to conceal. This invention also emphasized its evolving role as a practical tool, rather than just a weapon. Sasah Pestka, a Paramedic with more than twenty years on the mean streets of Chicago and very strong women in her own right, was the one whom stressed this recommendation. Sasha feels that all strong girls need carry a pocket knife due to the vast amount of times she found uses for hers. Miss Pestka states a knife is useful for many tasks such as opening boxes and cutting rope or even to protecting yourself from racist in Texas (it's a good story about her deployment to help folks during Hurricane Katrina). Here are just a few reasons your daughter should always have a pocket knife handy:

Every Day Carry (EDC)

Carrying a knife makes it easier to cut tape, cut string, cut trailing threads on clothing, open boxes, open clamshell packaging, cut/strip wires, prepare food like fruits and vegetables, open mail/envelopes, open food packaging, cut paper when scissors are absent, cut zip ties, cut tubing, remove tags from new clothing, or even for sentiment.

Emergency Preparedness/Survival

It's great to have a knife in case of an emergency or survival situation. Carrying a knife makes it easier to cut seat belt straps for extrication, create cloth bandages, cut rope, make kindling, scrape a fire steel, create a fire board and spindle, dig out a splinter, build a shelter, prepare wild game, collect wild edibles, make traps, carve utensils, make a spear, make an atlatl, and/or make feather sticks.

Self Defense

Lastly many people carry a knife for self-defense. I am a huge proponent of knowing how to defend yourself. Many people carry a knife as part of their self-defense carry. Law enforcement, body guards, soldiers, and security often have a knife in their gear. The one rule I have encountered that is always true is once a knife is introduced into a dispute, someone **WILL** get cut.

Final Thoughts

A knife has a place in every strong females pocket or purse. As parents of girls we must teach our daughters that it is ok for them to use the tools that are at hand and to always be prepared for any situation that comes their way. When this occurs then they will become truly strong like Sasha!!

CHAPTER 9

SEPTEMBER

You never know how strong you are, until being strong is your only choice.
Bob Marley

Tell your daughter "I love you" everyday

Words are powerful, and the word *love* might be the most powerful of them all. <u>When you hear that someone loves you, it can change everything, especially how you feel about yourself.</u> Words are especially impactful to our girls, who are still figuring out who they are. In their formative years, what you say to your daughter—or don't say—can make or break her. So in order for our girls to grow up strong we must tell them we love them every day.

Love Allows girls To Believe in Their Worth

I personally tell my daughter I love her frequently, first and foremost, because I do and even though I don't love every part of being a dad, I never stop loving her. I also tell her, because I believe that the words we speak to our children are heard by them, and it is with those words that they eventually form their own thoughts about themselves and feelings of self-worth.

As my daughter grows, I want that opinion of her to be nothing less than 100% loves and acceptance. I also believe that telling your daughter that you love her, as much as possible, will help her to become a better in countless ways rather than struggling with her self-identity.

Love for our daughters is unconditional

Too many girls grow up thinking that love is based on someone doing something that they agree with. I personally believe that it's not our disapproval so much that causes kids to keep things they're ashamed of from their parents when they get older, but their fear that will somehow impact their love for them. I don't want my daughter to believe this, because it's absolutely not true.

I also want to have an open and honest relationship with her that doesn't involve me turning a blind eye to anything she does wrong, just so that she doesn't think I don't love her. That's why I make an extra special effort to let my daughter know that I love her when she's done something wrong rather than taking my love away from her.

Make no misunderstanding that wrongdoing is met with proper discipline, a stern voice, and actions more than words, but it's always delivered with an "I love you." Love should be an unconditional expression that lets her know that even if I disapprove of an action, it hasn't changed the amount of love I have for her.

Final thoughts

Remember that when you hear that someone loves you, it can change everything, especially how you feel about yourself.

I've come to believe that the love of a parent is the baseline for how our girls learn to love. It's not absolute, but girls who grow up without love and affection may feel awkward when they enter relationships and have to give it.

When my daughter finds someone worth loving, I want her to know that it's okay to share her emotions and feelings with them, instead of having to overcome the hassle of learning to let their guard down. The only way I know how to accomplish this is by setting a good example myself for her to follow.

As much as I say 'I love you' regularly, I try to show how much love I have even more because after all, our girls pay attention to what we do more than what we say. Any chance I can sneak in a hug or a kiss, I do. I know that while those kisses and hugs are not finite; they will decrease in frequency as my child gets older.

So now is the time to shower her with all of my love and affection, so that when she grows older and starts to question who has her back, she'll never doubt that I do as her dad!

Eat Meals as a Family

Sadly, Americans rarely eat together anymore. In fact, according to a study by healthykids.gov,the average American eats one in every five meals in their car, one in four Americans eats at least one fast food meal every single day, and over 80 percent of American families report eating a single meal together less than five days a week. It's tragic that so many Americans are missing out on what could be meaningful time with their children the fact is that not eating together also has quantifiably negative effects both physically and psychologically on children.

According to a study by Michael Cambridge (2015), children who do not eat dinner with their parents at least twice a week were 40 percent more likely to be overweight compared to those who do. On the contrary, children who do eat dinner with their parents five or more days a week have less trouble with drugs and alcohol, eat healthier, show better academic performance, and report being closer with their parents than children who eat dinner with their parents less often, according to a study conducted by the National Center on Addiction and Substance Abuse at Columbia University.

The good news is that Children who eat regular family dinners also consume more fruits, vegetables, vitamins and micronutrients, as well as fewer fried foods and soft drinks. And the nutritional benefits keep paying dividends even after kids grow up: young adults who ate regular family meals as teens are less likely to be obese and more likely to eat healthily once they live on their own. Research by USDA (2016) has even found a connection between regular family dinners and the reduction of symptoms in medical disorders, such as asthma. The benefit might be due to two possible byproducts of a shared family meal: lower anxiety and the chance to check in about a child's medication compliance.

It isn't just the presence of healthy foods that leads to all these benefits. The dinner atmosphere is also important. Parents need to be warm and engaged, rather than controlling and restrictive, to encourage healthy eating in their children. When parents have dinner conversation with their children not only will they be healthier and happier but also smarter.

Family meals = smarter kids

Research by Shannon Bream (2017), found that for young children, dinnertime conversation boosts vocabulary even more than being read aloud to. The researchers counted the number of rare words – those not found on a list of 3,000 most common words – which the families used during dinner conversation. Young kids learned 1,000 rare words at the dinner table, compared to only 143 from parents reading storybooks aloud. Kids who have a large vocabulary read earlier and more easily.

A study by the National Association Healthy Children, found that a consistent association between family dinner frequency and academic performance. Adolescents who ate family meals five to seven times a week were twice as likely to get A's in school as those who ate dinner with their families fewer than two times a week.

Conclusion

Remember the real power of dinners lies in their interpersonal quality. If family members sit in stony silence, if parents yell at each other, or scold their kids, family dinner won't have positive benefits. Sharing a healthy dinner won't magically transform parent-child relationships however it could turn into something extraordinary. According to Anne Fishel, author of The Family Dinner Project, diner may be the one time of the day when a parent and child can share a positive experience – a well-cooked meal, a joke, or a story – and these small moments can gain momentum to create stronger connections away from the table.

Teacher your daughter something new everyday

Not only should the girls in our lives be strong physically and emotionally but also mentally. Many scientist believe that the "brain is like a muscle." Just like other muscles, you have to exercise the brain by learning new things. Yes, there is ample research which shows that learning helps build neuron connections and can stave off diseases like Parkinson's. But there is a lot more to learning new things than just making the brain stronger. The act of learning actually makes us happier.

As Belle Beth Cooper writes about in her post on "Why New Things Make Us Feel So Good", there is a section in the brain known as the SN/VTA.

The SN/VTA part of the brain is linked to the learning and memory parts, but it is best known as the "novelty center" because it lights up when exposed to new stimuli. You experience a rush of dopamine, which is one of the chemicals that motivate us towards rewards.

Here is what happens:

- You experience something new.
- The "novelty center" of your brain is activated.
- You get a rush of dopamine.

- Dopamine motivates you to follow through with the new thing.
- You get another rush of dopamine when you finish the activity.

It is no surprise then that research has found dopamine is closely linked to the learning process. In short, learning new things stimulates happiness chemicals in your brain. When your kid's brain is happy then they are one step closer to being extraordinary. Here is a step by step way to teach your daughter something new every day:

Pick a topic

Since there are literally billions of topics you could teach your girl about each day, the first step that needs to be taken is to have some organization and purpose to the daily learning process. For me personally I decided that I would narrow the subjects to three different categories; the first subject would be something that my daughter is interested in and enjoy talking about. For my daughter she loves the zoo and the nature center so the topic will be animals. I decided the second subject would be something that I enjoy which is football, more specifically the Green Bay Packers. The Third subject would be something simple yet something she could use in everyday life which is a new vocabulary word that they can apply in school.

I suggest picking subjects that your girls are fascinated with and that the topic is something that you and your child can bond over. I also suggest teaching your children something that can help them get ahead in school and life as well. It could be a subject that they are currently learning about or even a foreign language. Again, the key is making sure the subject is something that is enjoyable to talk about by both you and your girl and that this activity is something that you both look forward to each day.

Time and Place

Once a subject is chosen to be taught to your daughter the next step is to figure out both a time and place for the learning to take place on a consistent basis. For me, the time and place is when I'm driving her to school in the morning. So far my daughter and I usually talk about an animal for anywhere from 2 minutes to the whole 15 minute car ride. If the conversation only last for only a few minutes I then move on to the next subject Green Bay Packers Players. Since my daughter is younger this conversation doesn't last long and then finally we talk about a new word and what it means and how to use it in the sentence.

Besides the car ride to school other great times and places that could be used to teach your daughter something new is at the table while eating a meal also bath time or even right before you tuck them in for the night would be great times as well. Ideally use around 5 to 15 minutes to both teach and then allow for discussion. My daughter usually has a least one question that they ask about the subject.

If you are unable to see the girl in your life on a daily basis a great way to teach them something new each day is through emails or texts. For example each night you could email your grandchild a new type of Shark to learn about each day. Be sure to include pictures and videos attached in the email along with a few sentences about the subject.

Use Technology

We are lucky to live in the technology age, where all the information a parent would ever need is on our phones and computers. Just by doing a simple google search on a subject can bring endless amount of information right in front of us. Be sure to use all the tech resources out there such as YouTube and Wikipedia. Definitely do a web search on the subject you are teaching your children and make sure to use a many pictures and videos as possible. Remember many kids are visual learners so adding any kind of graphic information on your subject is a major plus.

Conclusion

By teaching the girl in your life something new every day you are making them stronger then you can imagine. Remember learning makes your daughter more interesting to their peers and also makes it easier for them to relate to more people. The more they know, the more likely they are to find something in common with others.

Practice makes perfect when it comes to our girls and learning. When our daughters are mastering new knowledge and skills, they build self-efficacy. Empowering is also a byproduct of learning something new every day. Learning gives your kids the information they need to make better informed decisions in life. Finally learning fuels creativity in our children. As Positive Psychology champion Vanessa King says, ideas come from seemingly unrelated things. Learning new things can trigger ideas in other areas

CHAPTER 10

OCTOBER

"I believe in being strong when everything seems to be going wrong. I believe that happy girls are the prettiest girls. I believe that tomorrow is another day, and I believe in miracles." — Audrey Hepburn

Teach our girls not to resent other people's success.

Today's world makes it hard for our girls not to resent other people's success. Spend two minutes on social media and you'll see how well everyone else seems to be doing. It could vacation photos from France that can remind your daughter how much money a friend may have. And not to mention the number of likes a friend receives on her posts may cause her to feel like she needs to be more popular. Bottom line is that researchers have found that envying your friends on Facebook actually leads to depression. And of course, resenting people's success in everyday life is even more harmful.

Here are some ways the girls in our lives can stop resenting other people's success:

Stop comparing to Other People

Saying things like, "Their house is nicer than ours," or "She's skinnier than I am," isn't a healthy way to measure your self-worth. And it's not a fair comparison. It's like comparing apples and oranges.

Don't Put-Down Other People's Accomplishments

Thinking, "He only got promoted because he kisses up to the boss," or "She only got that award because her family is rich," breeds feelings of resentment. You'll never become mentally stronger by diminishing someone else's accomplishments.

Practice acceptance. Acknowledge someone else's achievement without passing judgment.

Develop an Awareness of their Stereotypes

It's easy to make assumptions about successful people. But just because someone is rich, famous, or business-savvy doesn't mean he/she used unsavory methods to get there.

Be aware of the types of assumptions you make about people who are better off than you are. Focus on getting to know them as individuals before you draw sweeping generalizations.

Stop Emphasizing their Weaknesses

Sometimes it's easy to focus on your weaknesses and other people's strengths. But thinking that way will only cause you to become envious, and perhaps hopeless.

Be willing to acknowledge things you could improve upon, but don't magnify your shortcomings. Practice self-compassion and strive to do your best.

Quit Trying to Determine What's Fair

Sometimes, people have more luck than others. It's a fact of life. But focusing on what's fair or who is most deserving isn't a productive use of your time.

In fact, complaining about fairness can leave you feeling bitter. And those feelings of bitterness can become a huge stumbling block that will sabotage your efforts to reach your greatest potential.

Create Their Own Definition of Success

Remember that just because someone else has what you want, doesn't mean you can't have it too. But make sure you aren't just following in someone else's footsteps or chasing other people's dreams. Create your own definition of success and you'll be less threatened by people who are striving to reach their goals.

Final thoughts

Our daughters need to make sure that they keep their eyes on their own path. After all, every minute you spend thinking about other people reaching *their* dreams is a minute you didn't spend working on achieving your own.

Strong Girls have a VOICE in making decisions

We as parents must do our best to raise an assertive girl who isn't shy to use her voice. Teaching your daughter to have a voice and be assertive is an important life skill that may benefit her future. Experts say assertiveness skills can help your daughter's relationships—whether they are romantic ones or friendships, in work or school settings, or simply with themselves.

Here are a few simple ways parents can go about helping their daughters pick up these skills and feel empowered to share their voice as they grow.

Let Your Daughter Answer for Themselves

Whether it's greeting a friend you cross paths with on the street or ordering their own meal in a restaurant, let your girl speak for themselves. "Parents want to make life easy for their children, especially when they are shy, so they answer for them," says Marcie Beigel, BCBA-D, behavior specialist and founder of Behavior and Beyond in New York, where she provides individual therapy, parenting classes, and training. "Stopping this habit from the parent brings forward power and importance of the child's voice and encourages them to use it in new and varied situations."

Carve Out Time for Thoughtful Discussions

Create time each day to have thoughtful conversations with your daughter. Perhaps during meals or on a family walk, talk to your kids about topics that matter to your family and ask them what they think and wait for them to answer. Make sure that you be curious about her thoughts and ask questions such as, "Where did you learn that?" and "How did you come up with that thought?" or saying, "Interesting, tell me more."

Dr. Sarah Rosenberg agrees, adding that it's important to ask your daughter open-ended questions about the topics they bring up, even if they show resistance. Rather than just saying something along the lines of, "Wow, that's cool," tries to dig a little deeper and ask them a question about what they are saying. You can use statements like, "I wonder why..." or "I have noticed that..." This allows your daughter to think and begin to open up a bit more, advises Rosenberg.

Try Not to Judge Them

It's critical to leave judgment behind as much as possible. Remember that girls carefully decide when they are going to bring up topics that are hard, and when they feel they are being judged, they may shut down. It is important that when girls do try to bring up a topic, parents are able to listen without being judgmental. Parents, this means not asking questions that may provoke the child to be on the defense or say, 'Never mind.'"

If there is a moment in which your daughter does redact their statement, give it a moment and then acknowledge that you understand it can be hard to talk about certain things.

Give Your Child Choices Early On

Strawberries or blueberries? Which book before bed? What color winter coat to wear? These may seem like simple choices, but they can make a big impact. "Even these types of choices will help young girls get used to choosing and speaking up for what they want," says Kathryn Ely, J.D., a certified counselor and founder of Empower Counseling & Coaching in Birmingham, Alabama.

Avoid Labeling Your Daughter

Labeling girls or placing them into specific categories can hinder their confidence in big ways. "Children easily adapt the identity handed down to them by their parents, who can make it more difficult for a child or adolescent to find their voice and use it," says Ely.

Be supportive as they try and find their way and avoid comparing siblings. "Children really hang on to comments that parents think nothing of making, like calling one of your children 'the smart one' and the other child 'the funny one,'" explains Ely. "Instead, it would be much more helpful if the parent just complimented the child as doing something that was smart or saying something that was funny." That leaves each child open to growth and change instead of living up to and identifying with a label, she adds.

Help Them Strengthen Their Opinions

Using trusted resources, teach and show your daughter how to do research on any opinions she may have. If your daughter expresses that they think a vegetarian diet is the best way to go, you can research trusted websites together about vegetarian diets for kids. . Then, opt to discuss different diets and get a doctor's opinion, too. This way you thought about their opinion, your opinion, and got an expert opinion to discuss.

Having information to back up an opinion takes a feeling and transforms it into an informed thought, helping kids to become more assertive. Evidence, proof, and facts are often more persuasive. Looking at feelings and thinking critically to develop your opinion can help with the development of executive cognitive functioning—the ability to make reasoned decisions." Research shows good executive functioning comes with many benefits to boot, including lifelong achievement, quality of life, and health.

Encourage Change through Actions

Discuss how actions like volunteering and neighborhood cleanups can affect the community and the world—and then find ways to actively participate. When your daughter participates in a cause they are interested in or support, they understand the power of action and taking a stand. When this occurs the girls in our lives are one step to becoming truly strong.

Strong girls learn to like their dislikes

Our girls might have a part of their day they dislike, such as riding the bus to school or running lines at basketball practice. Or perhaps there's a point in their day that feels like a slog- after lunch or right when the alarm goes off. Our daughters might think there is nothing to appreciate during these moments. But maybe if they look closer, they might be surprised to find things they can be thankful for. Maybe the bus ride to school offers you time to listen to music that they love or maybe their post lunch tiredness gives them an opportunity to enjoy their favorite coffee (if old enough) The bottom line is we must teach our girls how to make these moments more bearable and maybe even fun.

The first step to learning to like your dislikes is to identify what part of the day is not fun and more importantly why? We as parents must sit down with our daughters and have an honest and open conversation to find out just why this part of the day sucks for our girl.

Once the "what, when and why" of the dislikes are established then the next step is to find the positive in that point of the day and turn the dislike into a like. This can be done by figuring out what this part of the day offers that other moments don't. Figuring this out may be a challenge but we as parents must step up and if needed really take the lead and put some effort into finding a positive spin on a dislike.

The final step in our daughters turning a dislike into a like is to reframe the way she thinks about it. The reframing a negative into a positive is something that truly all strong girls will need to master and with the help of great role models will be achieved.

CHAPTER 11

NOVEMBER

"A strong women alone is enough for this world, you do not have to prove anything to anybody." – Maya Angelou

Encourage your daughter to pursue a passion

One of the most important roles that parents have in the raising of their daughter is to help insure that they find something to be passionate about in life. We must provide our girls with an atmosphere that motivates them to learn and we must help in shaping their lifelong skills to find what they are passionate about. Research shows that regardless of the interests involved, a child is more likely to do well in academics when she has a passion in life. Here are other benefits of encouraging your daughter to follow their passions.

Pursuing Passions Releases Dopamine

When you force your girl to do something, they don't feel joy. When they do something that they want to do, however, their brain kicks into overdrive, releasing substantial amounts of dopamine. The feel-good chemical, dopamine makes your daughter feel joy and a sense of accomplishment. It also keeps them focused and encourages them to keep hard at work, developing their talents in any given area.

A girl that feels joy while doing a certain task will perform that task more often and become better at it. Any advances or accomplishments that come from their efforts will go a long way in increasing their self-esteem. Who doesn't want their child to feel good and to feel good about themselves?

Multiple Interests help your daughter Find Themselves

Self-discovery is a process that can take a lifetime, which is evident by the number of adults who are still trying to figure out who they are and what they're passionate about. By allowing your child to pursue multiple passions and hobbies, you can help them discover themselves much more quickly.

By engaging in multiple activities, your daughter will quickly discover what they like to do and what does not hold their interest for long, which will not only help them develop their own identity but also help them decide what they want to be when they grow up.

Passion-Based Learning Is Rooted in Science

Of all the learning models practiced today, passion-based learning is garnering some well-deserved respect. Passion-based learning involves finding what a child is passionate about and using that passion to inspire learning.

When a child is passionate about something, they will want to study it and will enjoy a greater understanding of the subject matter. More and more teachers are finding that passionate students are integral to student engagement.

Interests Will Keep Your daughter on the Straight and Narrow

When a girl gets bored, they are more likely to pursue or engage in behaviors that you would frown upon. A girl that is constantly engaged and busy, however, gets into less trouble and stays on that straight and narrow path.

Sports are one way that girls can burn off excess energy and stay out of trouble because sports keep children engaged. Interests, whether they are physical in nature or not, will also help your child learn self-discipline and goal setting.

Hobbies help your daughter Form Connections with Others

When your daughter pursues a hobby or activity that they're passionate about, they're more likely to share that knowledge with others and/or seek out others with the same interests. Their interest in a passion project could very well become the hub of their social circle.

By connecting with other like-minded individuals, your daughter can build relationships that could serve them well into adulthood and beyond. The right relationships may even open doors for your daughter in the future that you can only dream about now.

Now that we established how very important pursuing a passion is for our daughters, the next step is to take the steps needed to find and foster them. Here are some tips for parent to encourage their girl's passions:

Get out of the house

It's important to take your daughters out so they can see what's going on with their own eyes. From sporting to theatre events, or even a walk around a local historic castle, it's about getting out, seeing the world and being able to form an opinion about what they like.

Cultural exposure

Exposing girls to other cultures and language can be powerful. If you can afford it, this can be abroad. But it could simply be going to local cultural events and celebrations e.g. watching the Chinese New Year parade through a local Chinatown, trying language classes or checking out themed exhibitions. Exposing your girls to different cultures really helps to broaden their knowledge, spark their imaginations and develop their awareness of the wider world and how they fit in it.

Challenge yourselves as a family

Try something new every weekend. It's easy to fall into a pattern of repeating the same activities each week. In the future your daughter will say 'as a child I used to...' Help them write that future narrative, opening their eyes up to the possibilities.

Allow her to dream big

Girls' aspirations may seem far-fetched, but go on the journey with them. females aspirations should be encouraged, heard and valued as children with high aspirations show greater motivation and go on to have more positive life outcomes, including educational attainment and earnings in adulthood. So having aspirations at all is as important as them being realistic.

Remember: it's never too late to get started. Adolescence is a major developmental task where she really starts to consider and deliberately shape their identities; which, thankfully, continue to evolve as we get older.

It is as important to open up the eyes of a 5-year-old to the world as it is a 15-year-old. Adolescence is where self-limiting beliefs can creep in but this is where you, as parents, through conversation and opportunity can help to keep these beliefs at bay. Show your child the curiosities and opportunities that exist and can be sought out in the world.

When it comes to girls aspirations of what they want to be, parents play a huge role. What you and other family members do or want to do will influence your girls. From a young age, the professions they start to aspire to are often the ones they see in their immediate environment, so showing them other ideas will broaden their sphere. Similarly, if they could be influenced by negatives in their environment, help them see life beyond this by explicitly sharing your belief in them and showing them different examples

Final thoughts

Having worked for the Green Bay Packers for 15 years I was around a bunch of successful athletes and the one thing in common most bring up when talking about their parents is that When they were kids their parents always said the words: "I love watching you play." It's not about winning, it's not about losing. It's not about being "the best." So remember when you are helping your daughters find their passion say:

"I love watching you cook"

"I love watching you dance"

"I love watching you build those LEGO towers"

In the end, that may be the simplest, most effective way in the world to help nourish our girls' passions and have them become strong girls!

Foster skills for Independence – Cooking, Cleaning, Fixing Stuff

One moment you're holding your tiny newborn in your arms and the next you're driving her away to college. Time goes by quickly during parenthood. Over the course of a few years, our girls go from being completely dependent on us to living on their own. It leaves us, as parents, wondering: will they be ready to venture into the world without us.

As parents we must make sure that our girls can be independent. This doesn't mean that we just teach them to do laundry and make meals but also that they know how to problem-solve, handle failure, and generally act like a responsible adult. For some girls, it's just a matter of maturity. They're simply not developmentally ready to jump into independent living. For others, it's more a matter of preparation. They've never had the chance to exercise the skills needed to be independent. Over the years, adults have taken care of them – managed their schedule, cleaned their room, done their laundry or their dishes, the list goes on.

One of the greatest gifts we can give our daughters is to ensure they're self-sufficient when they leave home. Some kids will arrive at self-sufficiency on their own, but most need a little extra help to make their way. Similar to other skills (such as reading or math), the majority of kids need coaching and practice to achieve independence.

It's never too early to start coaching your kids towards self-sufficiency. In fact, the earlier you start the better! Keep in mind that many of the life skills that adults take for granted can take years for kids to learn.

If you've ever worried about your daughter being ready to go out into the world on their own, you aren't alone! Here are some simple things as parents you can do for fostering independence in your girls starting right now:

Learn How to Step Back

The first step to raising self-sufficient girls who will become independent young adults is to recognize that we're not doing our kids a favor by taking care of their every need. While our motive behind "doing" for our child may come from a place of love and a desire to see our children succeed, it can do more harm than good.

Managing our older daughters schedule, cleaning their rooms for them, or making sure they don't forget their homework, will ultimately handicap our children when it's time for them to exercise these skills on their own.

Instead, step back and ask yourself if the tasks you're performing for your child are something they're actually developmentally ready to do themselves. If the skill is age-appropriate, then start to hand them over to your child — focusing on one skill at a time so that it is not overwhelming to your daughter.

Take On the Mindset of a Coach

It's very easy to become frustrated when our girls aren't demonstrating the responsibility we expect from them. How many times do we need to remind them that dirty clothes belong in the hamper? Or to not forget their snow boots before leaving for school on Tuesday? We may wonder why these seemingly simple tasks seem impossible for our girls to master.

The danger with this is that we may criticize — explicitly or implicitly — our girls for their failures. <u>Anyone who feels criticized isn't likely to want to change their behavior or listen to further guidance from the person criticizing them.</u> It's important to keep in mind that it takes time for children to develop skills and some skills don't come naturally to every kid. Often children need our continued support for many years before they eventually demonstrate independence and responsibility.

Taking on the mindset of a coach can help. A good coach believes that the person he or she is coaching:

- Has potential to learn and grow
- Does not intentionally make mistakes
- Simply needs instruction to improve

Being supportive and respectful of where your child is in his or her developmental process will keep them open to receiving more guidance in the future.

Encourage Kids to Problem-Solve

Knowing how to problem-solve is a vital skill, as it equips children and adults with the ability to act independently in a variety of situations. One of the best ways to foster independence is to prioritize allowing girls to practice and fine-tune problem-solving while they're still at home.

Let's say your daughter forgot to submit her math homework today. It may be tempting to jump in and say "Well, if you had submitted it right when you finished it this never would have happened." (And let's face it; it takes a lot of willpower *not* to say this!)

Instead, you can build your daughter's problem-solving skills by asking questions to help her avoid a similar mistake in the future. For example, you could ask: "What do you think you could do next time so you won't forget to submit your homework?"

By prompting her with questions, she is not only more likely to come up with a good solution, but she'll also be much more likely to follow-through with the solution since it was her idea.

Get girls Started on Chores

One practical step parents can take to build a responsible mindset and foster independence is to have them do chores. Children who are given chores are more likely to have good relationships with family and friends, achieve academic and early career success and be self-sufficient, according to a study conducted at the University of Minnesota.

Chores not only teach children how to perform basic household tasks, they also teach a sense of working towards a common good (in this case, contributing to keeping the family home clean).

It's important, however, that girls feel included in the organization and execution of doing household chores, as opposed to being told that they must do them. For example, you could hold a family meeting and:

- Discuss how it's in everyone's interest to maintain a tidy and clean home
- Talk about how everyone (parents and kids) in the family does chores
- Make a list of which chores need to be done and discuss as a family who will do each
- Create a visual chart of the chores so no one "forgets" what they need to do

Here are some additional ideas for getting kids started on chores the right way. The key is to remember that this may take some effort upfront, but will vastly improve our chances of success in the long run.

Teach Girls Life Essentials Such As Money Management

Creating an environment for our girls where they can learn to problem-solve and exercise their independence is one of the most beneficial ways we can help them prepare for their adult lives. Girls can also benefit from learning specific, essential life skills; such as how to do laundry, how to cook, and perhaps most beneficial of all, how to manage money.

That last skill is especially important because most people enter adulthood with no experience in managing money. Few schools teach students how to budget, save, and understand credit; so it's often up to parents to teach their children.

One of the best ways to accomplish this is to give our girls a small amount of money to manage on their own and assign them some expenses to be responsible for. Young girls might receive three dollars each week and be responsible for purchasing craft supplies, Legos, or other toys. Teens might be made responsible for paying their cell phone bill, gas for the car, entertainment, and clothing.

This pairing of allowance and expenses provides girls with hands-on experience in determining how to budget, save and delay gratification to achieve goals.

Final thoughts

It takes dedication and a whole lot of patience to foster independence in girls. It can be frustrating in the moment when our girls have failed to make her bed for the third day in a row, or when our daughters hasn't properly planned her weekend to get all her homework done. It's so much easier to manage these tasks for our girls (not to mention we often do them better).

As parents, we must constantly remind ourselves of the long-term objective: to foster independence in our girls so that they will not only survive, but thrive when they're eventually out in the real world on their own. This will also make our girls one step closer to being truly strong!

Teach your girl to embrace motherhood

We must always remember that good parents raise future good parents. Not only do our actions show our daughters how to care for children, but they also impart to them the importance and dignity of motherhood. Today, motherhood is too often regarded as the lesser path for a woman. Many women are now told that babies can get in the way of dreams. A mother must teach her daughter that babies and dreams can go hand-in-hand.

Maybe more importantly girls who grow up to be good mothers make society a better place. A 2012 study from Washington University School of Medicine actually found that children who received warm, maternal nurturing in early childhood ended to develop a larger hippocampus- the learning, memory, and stress response center in the brain (Dryden, 2012). A mother like this holds many jobs. She acts as a teacher, a comforter, a nurse, and a mediator. Her job requires an understanding of medicine, psychology, math, management, cooking, cleaning, interior design, exceptional leadership skills, and undying patience to name a few. No mother is perfect, and this too can benefit a child, as they learn to deal with struggles and imperfections in life. Bottom line in order for Strong women to exist in the future, all girls must embrace and know the importance of motherhood.

CHAPTER 12

DECEMBER

You're truly strong women if your actions create a legacy that inspires others to dream more, learn more, do more and become more." – Dolly Parton

Teach your daughter not to expect immediate results

The world is becoming increasingly fast-paced. However, we can't get everything we want instantly. For instance, working on improving your relationship with your significant other, losing weight, starting a successful business… it all takes some time before we get the desired results. In order to raise strong girls we must teach them not to expect immediate results. We must teach our girls the old adage that good things come to those who wait. We must teach them that if they don't see immediate results, they shouldn't decide that this isn't working and give up. Finally we must teach the girls in our lives that they should not be always looking for shortcuts to do things.

Here are some more reasons why the girls in our lives expect immediate results:

Lack of patience

When we don't get the results we want right away, we give up or move on to the next thing believing that we're wasting our time and that something else out there will work faster.

Over-estimate our abilities

Sometimes we think highly of ourselves that we end up setting high expectations of how well we're going to do at any given task.

We might assume that we'll become the best performing worker within the first month of employment.

Or that we're able to lose thirty pounds in just two weeks. We end up feeling disappointed and discouraged when we don't get these expected results.

We underestimate how long it's going to take

It's easy to forget that personal change and growth don't move as fast as the technologies of these days. We incorrectly assume that everything can happen fast

The Problem with Expecting Immediate Results

Unrealistic expectations about how fast you're going to get results and how easy the change is going to be will likely set you up to fail and give up and this is the worst possible outcome for the girls in our lives to have.

Below are some other problems that can occur when you expect immediate results:

tempted to take shortcuts.
When you're not able to see much progress, you might be tempted

to take a shortcut. Someone who isn't seeing results from her diet might overdo it and go on a crash diet in order to speed up the process.

However crash diets can weaken your immune system and increase your risk of dehydration, heart palpitations, and cardiac stress, making it an unsafe way to lose weight.

Make the wrong judgment.

When your expectations aren't met, you may decide that it isn't working and that you shouldn't waste more time, while in reality, you might be so close to success.

Negative emotions.

When you can't see results, you're likely to become disappointed and frustrated. This can slow you down and maybe even be tempted to give up and never try again.

Don't Expect Immediate Results: How To Commit To The Long Haul?

#1. Create More Realistic Expectations

Unrealistic expectations can set up our girls to fail. It's important to make sure we foster expectations as realistic as possible if we want her to commit to the long haul.

To achieve that try the following:

1. **Don't overestimate how easy the change is going to be.** Acknowledge that doing something different and getting used to something new in your life is going to take some time.

2. **Avoid placing a definite time limit.** Don't create a definitive timeline for the change you want to make.

Even though some people would claim that establishing a good habit or breaking a bad habit takes about 21 days, reality can be different. It might take much longer than that to establish your desired change.

3. **Don't overestimate the effects of the change on the quality of your life.** Some people might believe that losing weight would make them feel good about themselves and they feel motivated to start dieting and exercising.

However, after a while, even when they've lost some weight, they can't feel the positive change their weight loss made on the quality of their life. They soon feel discouraged and might give up.

4. **Acknowledge That Progress Isn't Always Obvious**

Progress isn't always a straight line. Things can get worse before they can get better. The challenges that come with making a change can be discouraging. You might even believe that things were much better before. However, if you keep your sight on your long-term goals, it can get much easier to keep going.

To accurately measure your progress, ask yourself the following questions:

- What are the results that I can realistically expect within one week, one month, and one year?
- How will I know if what I'm doing is working and that I'm on track toward my goal?

5. **Practice Delaying Gratification**

Instant gratification is at the heart of many problems whether it was physical, mental, or even financial problems.

Someone might not be able to put down the alcohol even though it's causing him so many problems.

And while we might be good at delaying gratification in some areas of our lives, we might find it hard to do so in other areas.

Below are some strategies to help you delay gratification and stop expecting immediate results:

1. **Keep your eyes on your end goal.** When you keep your focus on your end goal, it becomes easier to find the motivation to keep going. Visualize yourself meeting your goal every morning to remind yourself of it.

2. **Resist temptations.** Create a plan that will help you stay away from temptation. If you're trying to stop overspending, try to stay away from shops that you usually tend to spend your money in, or only take with you the amount of money that you need when you go grocery shopping.

3. **Find ways to cope with feelings of impatience and frustration.** Just because you're frustrated, doesn't mean that you should give up. Expect these feelings and find healthy ways to cope with any negative feelings you might feel during the process of change.

4. **Celebrate small achievements.** You don't have to wait until you reach your goal before celebrating. Instead, create short-term goals and celebrate each milestone you reach.

5. **Pace yourself.** People who make changes in a short amount of time are likely going to go back to their old ways. Oftentimes, the best way to reach goals and maintain a change is to do it in a slow and steady pace. Reaching your goals and making a change requires strong willpower to resist temptations.

Establish realistic expectations for yourself and be willing to commit to the long haul and you'll increase your chances of reaching your goals.

Final Thoughts

As parents we must remember that when applying the ideas from this book that it will take time to see the girls in our lives become stronger. We must not expect immediate results and like always be role models and practice what we preach to our daughters. After all only when we our strong can our daughters become strong as well!

Be the person you want your daughter to become

I saved the most important secret for last. If you want your daughter to become a strong and independent woman, be one yourself. "Do as I say, not as I do" has never worked. Not in the entire history of the planet. The good news? It's never too late to start writing a new story. So, while you're teaching your daughter about strength, start finding it in yourself. When you tell her that she's beautiful because she makes you laugh, remind yourself that you're beautiful because you help others laugh. **In other words, turn all of these suggestions in the book around and apply them to yourself.**

I've never been prouder to be a parent. To raise my daughter in a world where anyone can be recognized, have a voice, can lead, and have an impact if they put in the effort no matter if they are male or female. I want to teach her that all her dreams and aspirations are within her reach. That she can accomplish anything she puts her mind to. I will teach her how important it is to not only take care of herself but of her community as well. I want to raise a strong, independent, and self-confident daughter, just like the woman that raised me.

Final Thoughts

"Mothers and fathers shape the future of the world, because they shape their children"

Strong girls grow up feeling secure in themselves. They learn to take action — making positive choices about their own lives and doing positive things for others. They think critically about the world around them. They express their feelings and acknowledge the feelings and thoughts of others in caring ways. Strong girls feel good about themselves and grow up with a "can-do" attitude. However the only way our girls can become truly strong is through good parenting and that is essentially what is book is all about.

The bottom line is parenting is the most important issue facing our society. According to Dr. Ann Harrison of Harvard's school of sociology, the actions of parents is single largest variable implicated in childhood illnesses and accidents; teenage pregnancy and substance misuse; truancy, school disruption, and underachievement; child abuse; employability; juvenile crime; and mental illness. These are all serious issues that can negatively affect the life of our daughters well into adulthood. This is why it is so important that you use the suggestions from this book to raise strong girls.

"Given the importance of parenting it is a sad fact that most girls spend an average of 41 hours per week in front of some type of screen (TV, computer, phone) but they only spend 7 hour per week with their parents." (Administration for children and families annual report, 2019) Unfortunately, many parents either don't or are afraid to spend one-on-one time with their daughters. Besides missing out on the fun, parents miss out on bonding time and a chance to establish emotional intimacy with their kiddos. <u>Please take the time and use the suggestions from this book to spend more time with your daughters every chance you get.</u>

As parents we must make sure we are looking at the bigger picture of how we raise our daughters will impact on what type of adults they become. According to the famous child phycologist Mary Ainsworth, the future of our society is shaped now by how we rear our children, and we need to take this duty more seriously. Society must admit the importance of being a parent. Moms and dads should not feel they are wasting their talents if they stay home to raise children. I personally feel much more needed and fulfilled as a stay at home dad than I have at any other life endeavor.

Remember that the world will only be as strong as its families, and families will only be as strong as its parents. Peace on our planet begins with peace in the home. The sustainable development of our societies depends on the work of moms and dads collaborating to help each other raise not just kids but fully and integrally developed adults. "Respect for human dignity and rights flows much more easily from the school of familial love" (Erickson 1967). Since the future of the world passes by way of families today, parents and future parents need to be prepared, supported and encouraged to carry out their indispensable role, individually and mutually as a committed dynamic duo through building strong parenting skills.

Parenting skills assist parents in leading children into healthy adulthood, influencing their development, and maintaining their negative and positive behaviors. One of the goals of this book is to build upon parenting skills. As a parent other than reading this amazing book you should try every day to find a way to strengthen the following:

1. Maintain consistency: Parents that institute regular routines see benefits in their children's behavioral patterns;

2. Utilize resources available to them: This could be in written form such as this book or even places like nature centers or other places that promote learning
3. Take an interest in their child's educational and early developmental needs
4. Keep open lines of communication about what their child is seeing, learning, and doing, and how these things are affecting them.
5. Parent-child relationship skills: quality time spent positive communications and delighted show of affection.
6. Encouraging desirable behavior: praise and encouragement, nonverbal attention, facilitating engaging activities.
7. Teaching skills and behaviors: being a good example, incidental teaching, communicating logical incentives and consequences.
8. Anticipating and planning: advanced planning and preparation for readying the child for challenges, finding out engaging and age-appropriate developmental activities

The bottom line is as parents in order to see our girls succeed we must be involved in our daughter's life. Being an involved parent takes time and is hard work, and it often means rethinking and rearranging your priorities. It frequently means sacrificing what you want to do for what your daughter needs to do. We must be there mentally as well as physically.

Parents can sometimes forget how important we are in the lives of our children.

We have so much control we have in shaping their confidence and self-image. And it all starts with trust, with believing our daughter is capable, even though setbacks, surprises and all the complications that come with growing up.

Trust empowers girls, whether it's in the classroom or in the world at large, and the process of developing trust starts earlier than you think. Infants who are securely attached to their parents — who feel they can trust and depend on them — avoid many behavioral, social, and psychological problems that can arise later. A child's fundamental sense of security in the world is based on their caregiver being someone they can rely upon.

Remember, trust is mutual.

The degree to which your daughter can trust you will become reflected in their own ability to trust. Studies show that girls rated as less trustworthy by their teacher's exhibit higher levels of aggression and lower levels of "prosocial behavior" such as collaborating and sharing. Distrust in girls has also been associated with their social withdrawal and loneliness.

If we don't feel trusted when we're kids — or if there isn't anyone close to us we can trust — we have difficulty getting over it. We grow up thinking we're not trustworthy, and we accept it as a character trait. Sad to say our girls become what they think they are, and they can suffer for it.

Always laugh together, spend time together, and connect positively every single day. Whether it's sitting down to play a fun board game, going for a bike ride, cooking, watching a movie, or just reading a good book together (or reading different books side-by-side, if your child is older), good parents spend time doing something fun and connecting with their girls in small and large ways every single day. Time truly flies when we are involved in our daughter's life. After all Mothers and Fathers shape the future of the world, because they shape their children.

Bonus

Father /daughter poems
By
Dr. Jon Kester

IT"S TOUGH ON A DAD
By Jon Kester

It's tough on a dad when his girl grows up,
when she no longer romps and frolics like a pup.
It's tough on a dad when his girl gets old,
when she no longer cuddles with him when it's cold.
It's tough on a dad when his girl gets tall,
when she's off with Cee-Cee and Lucy to the mall.
She no longer runs through the grass up to her knees,
Or roll in the piles of fresh fallen leaves.
It's tough on a dad when his girl gets tall,
when she's off to school, looking at boys in the hall.
It's tough on a dad when she has homework to do,
when she forgets to play as she used to.
It's tough on a dad when instead of going on wild adventures to the woods or fields or pond,
His daughter becomes a woman - and the woman is gone.

Father forgets for the 21st century
By Dr. Jon Kester

Listen Daughter, I am saying this as you are fast asleep, one little hand crumpled under your Disney Princess pillow and another around your favorite stuffed animal. I have come into your room alone. Just a few minutes ago, as I sat reading my texts, an overwhelming wave of remorse swept over me. Guilty, I came to your bedside.

There are things which I am thinking, daughter; your actions have made me angry. I yelled at you for using way to much shampoo in the shower. I got irritated at you for wanting to wear your favorite shirt that looked faded instead of all the nice new clothes in your closet. I called out furiously when you left your wet towel in the middle of the hall way.

At breakfast I found fault, too. You spilled milk all over the counter. You dropped your cereal all over the floor. You forgot to wash your hands after eating and gave me a hug which got my shirt all dirty. As you ran out the door to get on the bus you turned and waved and yelled, "Goodbye, Daddy!" I frowned, and said in reply, "keep those new shoes I just bought you clean!"

Then it began all over again late this afternoon. As I drove up the road I noticed you using the iPad listening to music outside. There was dirt on the screen. I humiliated you in front of you friends Lucy and Hannah by yelling at you and sending you to have a "time out" in the house. An IPad is expensive, and if you had to buy one you would be more careful!

Do you remember later, when I was checking my emails, how you came nervously, with sort of a hurt look in your eyes? I glanced up over my laptop, impatient at the interruption; you hesitated at the door. "What is it that you want?" I snapped. You said nothing, but ran across the room, threw your arms around my neck and kissed me, and said "Good night daddy. I love you. Then you were gone, quickly running up the stairs.

Well, daughter, it was shortly afterwards that I closed my laptop and a terrible sickening fear came over me. What has habit been doing to me? The habit of finding fault, or criticizing; this was my reward to you for being a child. It was not that I did not love you: it was that I expected too much of you. I had expectations for you of those of an adult.

There is so much that was good, fine and true in your character. The little heart of yours was as big as a football stadium. This was shown by your spontaneous impulse to rush in and kiss me good night. Nothing else mattered tonight.

Daughter, I have come to your beside in the darkness, I have knelt there, ashamed! I know that you would not understand these things which I have told you in the morning hours. Tomorrow I will be a real daddy! I will befriend you, suffer when you suffer and laugh when you laugh. I will bite my tongue when impatient words come. I will keep saying as if it were a ritual: "She is just a little girl" I am afraid I have envisioned you as an adult.

Yet as I see you now, daughter, lying asleep in your bed, I see that you are still my baby. It seems like just yesterday you were a newborn in your mother's arms, looking up at me with a crinkled forehead. I have asked too much, too much!

Instead of condemning and criticizing our children, perhaps would it be better to try to understand them, to try to figure out why they do what they do. That's a lot more beneficial than criticism; and it produces sympathy, tolerance and kindness, rather than contempt...!!!

BIBLIOGRAPHY

Abidin, R. R. (1992). The determinants of parenting behavior. *Journal of Clinical Child Psychology, 21*(4), 407-412. https://doi.org/10.1207/s15374424jccp2104_12

Abidin, R. R. (2012) *Parenting Stress Index-4 professional manual.* Lutz, FL: PAR, Inc.

Amato; Howard & Reeves (2018) Father involvement and self-reportparenting of children with attention deficit-hyperactivity disorder. *Journal of Consulting and Clinical Psychology, 65*(2), 337-342. doi:10.1037/0022-006X.65.2.337

Åsberg, K. K., Vogel, J. J., & Bowers, C. A. (2008). Exploring correlates and predictors of stress in parents of children who are deaf: Implications of perceived social support and mode of communication. *Journal of Child and Family Studies, 17*(4), 486-499. doi:10.1007/s10826-007-9169-7

Bailey, C. L., & Rose, V. C. (2011). Examining teachers' perceptions of twice exceptional students: Overview of a qualitative exploration. *Ideas and Research You Can Use: VISTAS,* 1-12.

Baldwin, K., Brown, R. T., & Milan, M. A. (1995). Predictors of stress in caregivers of attention deficit hyperactivity disordered children. *American Journal of Family Therapy, 23*(2), 149–160. doi:10.1080/01926189508251345

Bandura, A. (1977). Self-efficacy: Toward a unifying theory of behavioral change. *Psychological Review,*

Banks, M. L., (2018). The impact of complex trauma and depression on parenting: An exploration of mediating risk and protective factors. *Child Maltreatment,* 8(4), 334-349. https://doi.org/10.1177/1077559503257106

Becker, J. (2016). Clutter Free with Kids: 55, 83–96.

Belsky, J., Crnic, K., & Woodworth, S. (1995). Personality and parenting: Exploring the mediating role of transient mood and daily hassles. *Journal of Personality,* 63(4), 905-929. https://doi.org/10.1111/j.1467-6494.1995.tb00320.x

Berson, M.L (2015). The advocacy experiences of parents of elementary age, twice-exceptional children. *Gifted Child Quarterly, 37*(1), 1-16. https://doi.org/10.1177/0016986215569275

Bianco, M., & Leech, N. L. (2010). Twice-exceptional learners: Effects of teacher preparation and disability labels on gifted referrals. *Teacher Education and Special Education, 33*(4), 319-334. https://doi.org/10.1177/0888406409356392

Blanche, E. I., Diaz, J., Barretto, T., & Cermak, S. A. (2015). Caregiving experiences of Latino families with children with autism spectrum disorder. *American Journal of Occupational Therapy, 69*(5), 1-11. https://doi.org/10.5014/ajot.2015.017848

Bream, A.S. (2017). *Completing your qualitative dissertation: A road map from beginning to end.* Thousand Oaks, CA: Sage Publications. 151

Cambridge, M. (2015). Mothers' and fathers' attributions and beliefs in families of girls and boys with attention-deficit/hyperactivity disorder. *Child Psychiatry & Human Development, 39*(1), 85-99. doi:10.1007/s10578-007-0073-6

Comallie-Caplan, L. (2012). The apple doesn't fall far from the tree: Gifted parents parenting gifted children. *SENGVine Gifted Adult Edition.* Retrieved from https://sengifted.org/archives/articles/gifted-parents-parenting-gifted-children

Covington, M. K.,(2013). Parenting stress among caregivers of children with chronic illness: A systematic review. *Journal of Pediatric Psychology, 38*(8), 809-828. https://doi.org/10.1093/jpepsy/jst049

Creasey, G., & Reese, M. (1996). Mothers' and fathers' perceptions of parenting hassles: Associations with psychological symptoms, nonparenting hassles, and child behavior problems. *Journal of Applied Developmental Psychology, 17,* 393-406. https://doi.org/10.1016/s0193-3973(96)90033-7

Creswell, J. W. (2007). *Qualitative inquiry & research design: Choosing among five traditions.* Thousand Oaks, CA: Sage Publications.

Crnic, K., & Greenberg, M. (1990). Minor parenting stress with young children. *Child Development, 54,* 209–217. https://doi.org/10.2307/1130770

Cross, J. R., & Cross, T. L. (2015). Clinical and mental health issues in counseling the gifted individual. *Journal of Counseling & Development, 93*(2), 163-172. https://doi.org/10.1002/j.1556-6676.2015.00192.x 152

Cuva, A. (2014). Traversing the uncharted arena of computer assisted qualitative data analysis software: Mapping out QDA Miner 4.1 as a first-time user. *The Qualitative Report, 19*(19), 1-4.

Daniels, S., & Piechowski, M. M. (Eds.) (2009). *Living with intensity: Understanding the excitability, sensitivity, and emotional development of gifted children, adolescents, and adults.* Scottsdale, AZ: Gifted Potential Press.

Dare, L., & Nowicki, E. A. (2015). Twice-exceptionality: Parents' perspectives on 2E identification. *Roeper Review, 37,* 208-218. doi:10.1080/02783193.2015.1077911

Deater-Deckard, K. (2004). *Parenting stress.* New Haven, CT: Yale University Press.

Deault, L. C. (2010). A systematic review of parenting in relation to the development of comorbidities and functional impairments in children with attentiondeficit/ hyperactivity disorder (ADHD). *Child Psychiatry and Human Development, 41*(2), 168-192. doi:10.1007/s10578-009-0159-4

Detmer, James. (2018). Responsible fathering: An overview and conceptual framework. *Journal of Marriage and Family, 60,* 277-292. doi:10.2307/353848

Duhigg, Charles(2009). The power of Habit: Implications for parent–child relationships and prevention research. *Clinical Child and Family Psychology Review, 12*(3), 255-270.
153

Elman,.A. J, (2011). Beyond internal and external: A dyadic theory of relational attributions. *The Academy of Management Review, 36*(4), 731-753. https://doi.org/10.5465/amr.2011.65554734

Engram, H. Thomas. (2020). Relationships between maternal parenting stress and child disruptive behavior. *Child & Family Behavior Therapy, 14*(4), 1-9. https://doi.org/10.1300/j019v14n04_01

Fischer, M. (1990). Parenting stress and the child with attention deficit hyperactivity disorder. *Journal of Clinical Child Psychology, 19*(4), 337–346. https://doi.org/10.1207/s15374424jccp1904_5

Folkman, S., Lazarus, R. S., Gruen, R. J., & DeLongis, A. (1986). Appraisal, coping, health status, and psychological symptoms. *Journal of Personality and Social Psychology, 50*(3), 571-579. doi:10.1037/0022-3514.50.3.571

Foster, S. David. (2018). Finding and serving twice exceptional students: Using triaged comprehensive assessment and protections of the law. In S. B. Kaufman (Ed.) *Twice exceptional: Supporting and educating bright and creative students with learning difficulties* (pp. 19-47). New York, NY: Oxford University Press.

Gelbs, J.S. (2003). Understanding reliability and validity in qualitative research. *The Qualitative Report, 8*(4), 597-606.

Grant, B. A., & Piechowski, M. M. (1999) Theories and the good: Toward child-centered gifted education. *Gifted Child Quarterly, 43*(1), 4-12. https://doi.org/10.1177/001698629904300102
154

Gross, M. (2004). *Exceptionally gifted children* (2nd Ed.). London, England: Routledge Falmer.

Grossman, F. K., Pollack, W. S., & Golding, E. (1988). Fathers and children: Predicting the quality and quantity of fathering. *Developmental Psychology, 24*(1), 82-91. doi:10.1037/0012-1649.24.1.82

Gupta, V. B. (2007). Comparison of parenting stress in different developmental disabilities. *Journal of Developmental & Physical Disabilities, 19*(4), 417–425. doi:10.1007/s10882-007-9060-x

Harrison J. A. (2018). Maternal positive parenting style is associated with better functioning in hyperactive/inattentive preschool children. *Infant and Child Development, 20*(2), 148–161. doi:10.1002/icd.682

Hurt, Karin. (2019). What we know about the early selection and training of leaders. *Teachers College Record, 40,* 575-592.

Individuals with Disabilities Education Improvement Act of 2004, 108 U.S.C. §§ 108- 446 (West, 2004).

Johnston, C., & Mash, E. J. (2001). Families of children with attentiondeficit/ hyperactivity disorder: Review and recommendations for future research. *Clinical Child and Family Psychology Review, 4*(3), 183–207. doi:10.1023/A:1017592030434 155

Jolly, J. L., & Matthews, M. S. (2012). A critique of the literature on parenting gifted learners. *Journal for the Education of the Gifted, 35*(3), 259-290. https://doi.org/10.1177/0162353212451703

Jolly, J. L., Matthews, M. S., & Nester, J. (2012). Homeschooling the gifted: A parent's perspective. *Gifted Child Quarterly, 57*(2), 121-134. https://doi.org/10.1177/0016986212469999

Kadesjö, C., Stenlund, H., Wels, P., Gillberg, C., & Hägglöf, B. (2002). Appraisals of stress in child-rearing in Swedish mothers of pre-schoolers with ADHD: A questionnaire study. *European Child & Adolescent Psychiatry, 11*(4), 185–195. doi:10.1007/ s00787-002-0281-3

Kane, M. (2013) Parent lore: Collected stories of asynchronous development. In C. S. Neville, M. M. Piechowski, & S. S. Tolan (Eds.) *Off the charts: Asynchrony and the gifted child* (pp. 226-259). Unionville, NY: Royal Fireworks Press.

Karpinski, R. I., Kolb, A. M. K., Tetreault, N. A., & Borowski, T. B. (2017). High intelligence: A risk factor for psychological and physiological overexcitabilities. *Intelligence, 66*(1), 8-23. https://doi. org/10.1016/j.intell.2017.09.001

Kaufman, S. B. (Ed.) (2018). *Twice exceptional: Supporting and educating brought and creative students with learning difficulties.* New York, NY: Oxford University Press.
156

Kazdin, A. E., & Wassell, G. (2000). Predictors of barriers to treatment and therapeutic change in outpatient therapy for antisocial children and their families. *Mental Health Services Research, 2*(1), 27-40.

Kazdin, A. E., & Whitley, M. K. (2003). Treatment of parental stress to enhance therapeutic change among children referred for aggressive and antisocial behavior. *Journal of Consulting and Clinical Psychology, 71*(3), 504-515. https://doi.org/10.1037/0022-006x.71.3.504

Kearney, K. (2013). Life in the asynchronous family. In C. S. Neville, M. M. Piechowski, & S. S. Tolan (Eds.) *Off the charts: Asynchrony and the gifted child* (pp. 211-225). Unionville, NY: Royal Fireworks Press.

Knott, L. J. (2020). Predictors of boys' ADHD symptoms from early to middle childhood: The role of father–child and mother–child interactions. *Journal of Abnormal Child Psychology, 40*(4), 569-581. doi:10.1007/s10802-011-9586-3

Lamb, M. E. (2010). *The role of the father in child development.* Hoboken, NJ: John Wiley & Sons.

Lange, G., Sheerin, D., Carr, A., Dooley, B., Barton, V., Marshall, D.,... Doyle, M. (2005). Family factors associated with attention deficit hyperactivity disorder and emotional disorders in children. *Journal of Family Therapy, 27*(1), 76–96. doi:10.1111/j.1467-6427.2005.00300.x
157

Latz, A. O., & Adams, C. M. (2011). Critical differentiation and the twice oppressed: Social class and giftedness. *Journal for the Education of the Gifted, 34*(5), 773-789. https://doi.org/10.1177/0162353211417339

Lazarus, R. S. (2006). *Stress and emotion.* New York, NY: Springer Publishing.

Lazarus, R. S., & Folkman, S. (1984). *Stress, appraisal, and coping.* New York, NY: Springer Publishing Company. Lombardi, D. V. (2004). *Different minds: Gifted children with AD/HD, Asperger syndrome, and other learning deficits.* London, England: Jessica Kingsley Publishers.

Makel, M. C., Kell, H. J., Lubinski, D., Putallaz, M., & Benbow, C. P. (2016). When lightning strikes twice: Profoundly gifted, profoundly accomplished. *Psychological Science, 27*(7), 1004-1018. https://doi.org/10.1177/0956797616644735

Manning, J., & Kunkel, A. (2014). Making meaning of meaning-making research: Using qualitative research for studies of social and personal relationships. *Journal of Social and Personal Relationships, 31*(4), 433-441. https://doi.org/10.1177/0265407514525890

Marshall.A.S (2019). Determinants of parenting stress: Illustrations from families of hyperactive children and families of physically abused children. *Journal of Clinical Child Psychology, 19*(4), 313-328. doi:10.1207/s15374424jccp1904_3

158

Maxwell, E. (1998). "I can do it myself!" Reflections on early self-efficacy. *Roeper Review, 20*(3), 183-187. https://doi.org/10.1080/02783199809553888

McCleary, L. (2002). Parenting adolescents with attention deficit hyperactivity disorder: Analysis of the literature for social work practice. *Health & Social Work, 27*(4), 285–292. doi:10.1093/hsw/27.4.285

Merrill, J. (2012). *If this is a gift, can I send it back?: Surviving in the land of the gifted and twice exceptional.* Ashland, OR: GHF Press.

Mueller, A. K., Fuermaier, A. B., Koerts, J., & Tucha, L. (2012). Stigma in attention deficit hyperactivity disorder. *ADHD attention deficit and hyperactivity disorders, 4*(3), 101-114.

Miller, J. B., & Stiver, I. P. (1997). *The healing connection: How women form relationships in therapy and in life.* Boston, MA: Beacon Press.

Modesto-Lowe, V., Danforth, J. S., & Brooks, D. (2008). ADHD: Does parenting style matter? *Clinical Pediatrics, 47*(9), 865–872. doi:10.1177/0009922808319963

Morelock, M. J. (1992). Giftedness: The view from within. *Understanding Our Gifted, 4*(3), 11-15.

Morelock, M. J. (1996). On the nature of giftedness and talent: Imposing order on chaos. *Roeper Review, 19*(1), 4-12. https://doi.org/10.1080/02783199609553774 Morgan, J., Robinson, D.,

& Aldridge, J. (2002). Parenting stress and externalizing child behaviour. *Child & Family Social Work, 7*(3), 219-225. https://doi.org/10.1046/j.1365-2206.2002.00242.x
159

Moustakas, C. (1994). *Phenomenological research methods.* Thousand Oaks, CA: Sage Publications.

Mudrak, J. (2011). 'He was born that way': Parental constructions of giftedness. *High Ability Studies, 22*(2), 199-217. https://doi.org/10.1080/13598139.2011.622941

Neece, C. L., Green, S. A., & Baker, B. L. (2012). Parenting stress and child behavior problems: A transactional relationship across time. *American Journal on Intellectual and Developmental Disabilities, 117*(1), 48-66. https://doi.org/10.1352/1944-7558-117.1.48

Neumann, L. C. (2008). No one said it was easy: Challenges of parenting twiceexceptional children. In Gosfield, M. (Ed.), *Expert approaches to support gifted learners: Professional perspectives, best practices and positive solutions* (pp. 269–276). Minneapolis, MN: Free Spirit Press.

Neville, C. S., Piechowski, M. M., & Tolan, S. S. (Eds.) (2013) *Off the charts: Asynchrony and the gifted child.* Unionville, NY: Royal Fireworks Press.

No Child Left Behind (NCLB) Act of 2001, 20 U.S.C.A. § 6301 et seq. (West, 2003).

Oakland, J. (2018). Boys will be boys: Fathers' perspectives on ADHD symptoms, diagnosis, and drug treatment. *Harvard Review of Psychiatry, 11*(6), 308-316. doi:10.1080/714044393

Oswald, I. (2014). Doing their jobs: Mothering with Ritalin in a culture of mother-blame. *Social Science & Medicine, 59*(6), 1193-1205. https://doi.org/10.1016/j.socscimed.2004.01.011

Owens, David. (2018). A structural modeling approach to the understanding of parenting stress. *Journal of Clinical Child Psychology, 29*(4), 615-625. https://doi.org/10.1207/s15374424jccp2904_13

Palmer R.M. (2013). The influence of primary caregivers in fostering success in twice-exceptional children. *Gifted Child Quarterly, 57*(4), 263-274. https://doi.org/10.1177/0016986213500068

Palson, Diana. (2011). Meaning, coping, and health and well-being. In S. Folkman (Ed.) *Oxford handbook of stress, health, and coping* (pp. 227-241). New York, NY: Oxford University Press. 160

Patton, M.Q. (2014). *Qualitative research & evaluation methods: Integrating theory and practice.* Thousand Oaks, CA: SAGE Publications.

Pelham, W., & Lang, A. (1999). Can your children drive you to drink? Stress and parenting in adults interacting with children with ADHD. *Alcohol Research & Health, 23*(4), 292–298.

Pew Study. (2018). Myth 17: Gifted and talented individuals do not have unique social and emotional needs. *Gifted Child Quarterly, 53*(4), 280-282. https://doi.org/10.1177/0016986209346946

Peterman, A. J. (2016). Bullying and the gifted: Victims, perpetrators, prevalence, and effects. *Gifted Child Quarterly, 50*(2), 148-168. https://doi.org/10.1177/001698620605000206

Petit, J.J. (2020). Where's poppa? The relative lack of attention to the role of fathers in child and adolescent psychopathology. *American Psychologist, 47*(5), 656-664. doi:10.1037/0003-066X.47.5.656

Piechowski, M. M. (2014). *"Mellow out," they say. If I only could: Intensities and sensitivities of the young and bright* (2nd ed.). Unionville, NY: Royal Fireworks Press.

Podolski, C. L., & Nigg, J. T. (2001). Parent stress and coping in relation to child ADHD severity and associated child disruptive behavior problems. *Journal of Clinical Child Psychology, 30*(4), 503–513. https://doi.org/10.1207/s15374424jccp3004_07
161

Postma, M. (2017). *The inconvenient student: Critical issues in the identification and education of twice-exceptional students.* Unionville, NY: Royal Fireworks Press.

Power, T. G., & Hill, L. G. (2010). Individual differences in appraisal of minor, potentially stressful events: A cluster analytic approach. *Cognition and Emotion, 24*(7), 1081-1094. https://doi.org/10.1080/02699930903122463

Prior, S. (2013). Transition and students with twice exceptionality. *Australasian Journal of Special Education, 37*(1), 19. https://doi. org/10.1017/jse.2013.3

Randall, A. K., & Bodenmann, G. (2009). The role of stress on close relationships and marital satisfaction. *Clinical Psychology Review, 29*, 105-115. https://doi.org/10.1016/j.cpr.2008.10.004

Raphael, J. L., Zhang, Y. Y., Liu, H. H., & Giardino, A. P. (2010). Parenting stress in US families: Implications for paediatric healthcare utilization. *Child: Care, Health and Development, 36*(2), 216-224. doi:10.1111/j.1365-2214.2009.01052.x

Robertson S.A. (2018). An operational definition of twiceexceptional learners: Implications and applications. *Gifted Child Quarterly, 58*(3), 217-230. https://doi.org/10.1177/0016986214534976

Saldaña, J. (2009). *The coding manual for qualitative researchers.* Thousand Oaks, CA: Sage Publications.

Sheeran, T., Marvin, R. S., & Pianta, R. (1997). Mothers' resolution of their childs's diagnosis and self-reported measures of parenting stress, marital relations, and

162

social support. *Journal of Pediatric Psychology, 22*(2), 197-212. https://doi.org/10.1093/jpepsy/22.2.197

Silverman, L. K. (1990). Social and emotional education of the gifted: The discoveries of Leta Hollingworth. *Roeper Review, 12*(3), 171-178. https://doi.org/10.1080/02783199009553265

Silverman, L. K. (1997). The construct of asynchronous development. *Peabody Journal of Education, 72*(3-4), 36-58. https://doi. org/10.1207/s15327930pje7203&4_3

Silverman, L. K. (1998). Through the lens of giftedness. *Roeper Review, 20*(3), 204-210.

Silverman, L. K. (2002). Asynchronous development. In M. Neihart, S. M. Reis, N. M. Robinson, & S. M. Moon (Eds.) *The social and emotional development of gifted children: What do we know?* (pp. 31-50). Waco, TX: Prufrock Press.

Silverman, L. K.. & Kearney, K. (1989). Parents of the extraordinarily gifted. *Advanced Development, 1*, 41-56.

Silverman, L. K., & Miller, N. B. (2009). A feminine perspective of giftedness. In L. V.

Silvestri.R.K. (2018). Stress, coping, and social support processes: Where are we? What next? *Journal of Health and Social Behavior,* (Extra issue), 53-79. https://doi.org/10.2307/2626957

Shavinina (Ed.), *International handbook on giftedness* (pp. 99-128). Amsterdam: Netherlands: Springer.

Singer, L. (2000). If giftedness = asynchronous development, then gifted/special needs = asynchrony3. In K. Kay (Ed.), *Uniquely gifted: Identifying and meeting the needs of twice-exceptional students* (pp. 44-46). Gilsum, NH: Avocus Publishing Inc.
163

Spicer, P. (2007). Commentary: From fathering to parenting and back again. *Applied Developmental Science, 11*(4), 203-204. doi:10.1080/10888690701762084

Spratt, E. G., Saylor, C. F., & Macias, M. M. (2007). Assessing parenting stress in multiple samples of children with special needs (CSN). *Families, Systems, & Health, 25*(4), 435-449. doi:10.1037/1091-7527.25.4.435

Stewart, D., & Mickunas, A. (1974). *Exploring phenomenology: A guide to the field and its literature.* Athens, OH: Ohio University Press.

Theule, J., Wiener, J., Rogers, M. A., & Marton, I. (2011). Predicting parenting stress in families of children with ADHD: Parent and contextual factors. *Journal of Child and Family Studies, 20*(5), 640–647. doi:10.1007/s10826-010-9439-7
164

Tieso, C. L. (2007). Patterns of overexcitabilities in identified gifted students and their parents: A hierarchical model. *Gifted Child Quarterly, 51*(1), 11-22. https://doi.org/10.1177/0016986206296657

Trépanier, C. (2015). *Educating your gifted child: How one public school teacher embraced homeschooling.* Olympia, WA: GHF Press.

Tzang, R. F., Chang, Y. C., & Liu, S. I. (2009). The association between children's ADHD subtype and parenting stress and parental symptoms. *International Journal of Psychiatry in Clinical Practice, 13*(4), 318-325. https://doi.org/10.3109/13651500903094567

Van der Oord, S., Bögels, S. M., & Peijnenburg, D. (2012). The effectiveness of mindfulness training for children with ADHD and mindful parenting for their parents. *Journal of Child and Family Studies, 21*(1), 139-147. https://doi.org/10.1007/s10826-011-9457-0

Van de Weijer-Bergsma, E., Formsma, A. R., de Bruin, E. I., & Bögels, S. M. (2012). The effectiveness of mindfulness training on behavioral problems and attentional functioning in adolescents with ADHD. *Journal of Child and Family Studies, 21*(5), 775-787. https://doi.org/10.1007/s10826-011-9531-7

165

Van Manen, M. (1990). *Researching lived experience: Human science for an action sensitive pedagogy.* Albany, NY: State University of New York Press.

Van Manen, M. (2014). *Phenomenology of practice: Meaning-giving methods in phenomenological research and writing.* Walnut Creek, CA: Left Coast Press.

Vialle, W. (2017). Supporting giftedness in families: A resources perspective. *Journal for the Education of the Gifted, 40*(4), 372-393. https://doi.org/10.1177/0162353217734375 Webb, J., Meckstroth, E., & Tolan, S. (1982). *Guiding the gifted child: A practical source for parents and teachers.* Columbus, OH: Ohio Psychology Publishing Company.

Weiner, B. (1985). An attributional theory of achievement motivation and emotion. *Psychological Review, 92*(4), 548-573. doi:10.1037/0033-295X.92.4.548

Weiner, B. (2000). Intrapersonal and interpersonal theories of motivation from an attributional perspective. *Educational Psychology Review, 12*(1), 1-14.

Wells, C. (2017). The primary importance of the inner experience of giftedness. *Advanced Development, 16*, 95-113.

Whalen, C. K., Odgers, C. L., Reed, P. L., & Henker, B. (2011). Dissecting daily distress in mothers of children with ADHD: An electronic diary study. *Journal of Family Psychology, 25*(3), 402. https://doi.org/10.1037/a0023473

Yehuda, R., Halligan, S. L., & Grossman, R. (2001). Childhood trauma and risk for PTSD: Relationship to intergenerational effects of trauma, parental PTSD, and 166 cortisol excretion. *Development and Psychopathology,* *13,* 733-753. https://doi.org/10.1017/s0954579401003170 1

67

Printed in the United States
by Baker & Taylor Publisher Services